Praise for A New Oracle of Kabbalah

"Jewish sages teach that each letter of the Hebrew alphabet is an awesome universe. Richard Seidman gently guides readers to explore the use of these letters to open mysterious gates of wisdom hidden within each one of us. *Oracle of Kabbalah* is an excellent tool for discovering the teachings of our own souls and is highly recommended."

–Rabbi David A. Cooper, author of *God is a Verb*

"These cards, grounded in ancient mystical knowledge, offer many doorways to the great mysterious, and the power of our own personal truth. To experience them is to realize the infinite depth and exquisite beauty of creation."

–David Carson, co-author of *The Medicine Cards*

"You don't have to be Jewish to love *Oracle of Kabbalah*. Richard Seidman has made the ancient wisdom and power of the Hebrew letters accessible to us all, so we can use it to help us better deal with the challenges of modern life."

–Monte Farber and Amy Zerner, authors of *The Enchanted Tarot*

"Seidman's *Oracle of Kabbalah* is a feast of honey, humor, cultural diversity, and an outrageous insistence on hope. Though well rooted in indigenous Jewish understandings, a thousand flowers of the world's teachers make this personal divination style one that promotes the Divine in Nature and community without losing the nobility of the individual."

–Martín Prechtel, author of *The Smell of Rain on Dust: Grief and Praise*

"In these wide-ranging, mystical, sometimes fanciful meditations on the letters of the Hebrew alphabet, Richard Seidman introduces the reader to a contemporary installment of both Judaism's millennial love affair with the letters of the Hebrew alphabet and a clever invitation to enter the conversation."

–Rabbi Lawrence Kushner, author of *The Book of Letters*

"Richard Seidman offers us a direct, clear, and practical approach to the Divine Mystery. His understanding of the Hebrew Aleph Beit and his guidance in interpreting each letter ignites an inner lamp that can illumine the most shadowed corners of the soul."

–Rabbi Rami M. Shapiro, author of *The Way of Solomon*

A New Oracle of Kabbalah
Mystical Teachings of the Hebrew Letters

To Judah,

In honor of the spiralling voices of the Holy,

Blessings,

A New Oracle of Kabbalah
Mystical Teachings of the Hebrew Letters

[signature]

RICHARD SEIDMAN
Foreword by Rabbi Rami M. Shapiro

White Cloud Press
Ashland, Oregon

AUTHOR'S NOTE

With gratitude to the trees of this world, the author will donate a portion of the profits of each book to Friends of Trees in Portland, Oregon, USA, to support the planting of new trees.

White Cloud Press books may be purchased for educational, business, or sales promotional use. For information, please write:

Special Market Department
White Cloud Press
PO Box 3400
Ashland, OR 97520
Website: www.whitecloudpress.com

Cover art and Hebrew calligraphy by Shoshannah Brombacher
Cover and interior design by Christy Collins, C Book Services

Printed in the United States

First edition: 2015
15 16 17 18 19 10 9 8 7 6 5 4 3 2 1

Library of Congress Cataloging-in-Publication Data
Seidman, Richard, author.
 A new oracle of Kabbalah : mystical teachings of the Hebrew letters / Richard Seidman.
   pages cm
 "This edition of Oracle of Kabbalah is a revised and expanded version of the book that was first published in 2001"--Preface.
  ISBN 978-1-935952-82-4 (paperback)
1. Hebrew language--Alphabet--Religious aspects--Judaism. 2. Cabala. 3. Spiritual life--Judaism. I. Title.
PJ4589.S418 2015
492.4'11--dc23
                 2015025633

To my father, Herbert Seidman, and my mother, Phoebe Seidman. May their memories be blessings.

To Aryeh Hirschfield, beloved rebbe of blessed memory.

To all our ancestors, no matter their tribes or original homelands, whose indigenous voices were silenced, but whose songs and stories still might echo through us.

And, with all my love, to Rachael Resch.

CONTENTS

ACKNOWLEDGMENTS

Abby Layton's inspiring example and generous spirit enabled me to find a Jewish path. This book would not exist if not for her influence.

I am grateful to Rabbi Aryeh Hirschfield, of blessed memory, for his initial inspiring presence and his continued guidance. For months, during the rainy Oregon winter, he and I would meet each week to read through my manuscript chapter by chapter. Rabbi Aryeh helped correct the Hebrew, clarified confusing points, and offered many helpful suggestions.

I thank my wife, Rachael Resch, for unfailing love, staunch support, wise perspective, brilliant insights, skillful editing, artistic vision, and for happy times.

I am grateful for the love and support of my mother, Phoebe Seidman, and my father, Herbert Seidman. May they both rest in peace.

Ilan Shamir's enthusiasm and perspective helped guide the early writing. Many other friends provided important feedback and encouragement, including Gordon Quinlan, John Ciminello, Ruth Resch, Nelson Foster, Donna Redisch, Aki Fleshler, Alon Raab, Hank Stratton, Ron Marson, Pat Ferris, and Steve Berman. Howard Lanoff, Babs Smith, Pat Ciminello, and Sharon Dvora were other stalwart supporters. I thank them all for their assistance and friendship.

I am grateful to my teachers Robert Aitken, Nelson Foster, Martín Prechtel, Paul Richards, and Stephen Victor. Their influence pervades these pages and my life.

Deborah and Rabbi David Zaslow have been good friends and supporters.

Thank you to Rabbi Julia Melanie Vaughns for her deep knowledge of the Hebrew letter mysteries and generous sharing of her expertise and wisdom.

I offer great gratitude to Shoshannah Brombacher for her intimacy with the Hebrew letters and for her beautiful artwork that graces the book cover and cards.

Deep thanks to Rabbi Rami Shapiro for his profound Foreword.

I appreciate proofreader Jill Bailin and her meticulous attention to detail.

Thank you to Steve Scholl and White Cloud Press for helping bring this new edition out into the world.

Thank you to all the humans I have forgotten to thank, to my ancestors, to the Angel of Writing, to the holy Hebrew letters themselves and their descendants, the letters of the Latin alphabet, and to all the many known and unknown beings and forces who have conspired to sing us into life and sing this project into life.

BUYING OR MAKING YOUR OWN
HEBREW LETTER DECK

Oracle of Kabbalah was originally conceived of and published as a book and card divination set. If you would like to purchase a deck of Hebrew letter cards to accompany this book, please go to www.whitecloudpress.com or http://tinyurl.com/oracle-deck.

If you prefer to create your own set of Hebrew letter cards, visit http://tinyurl.com/make-your-own-cards.

You can print the letters directly onto card stock or glue them onto cards. Or you can send the file to a print shop and have them print, cut, and laminate the cards for you.

Perhaps the easiest alternative is to simply draw each letter by hand and write its name on an index card.

If you have any questions or comments about this process, please contact me at info@oracleofkabbalah.com.

Thanks,
Richard Seidman

FOREWORD TO *A NEW ORACLE OF KABBALAH* BY RABBI RAMI M. SHAPIRO

Language is a vehicle of creation. It lifts something out of nothing, and in doing so infuses it with meaning.

This is what Helen Keller discovered when Anne Sullivan continually spelled the word *w-a-t-e-r* on her palm as she pumped actual water over her hand. This is what Torah reveals when she says: *In the beginning of God's creating sky and earth, the earth was formless and barren, darkness alone covered the deep, and God's breath quivered over the surface of the waters, and God said…* (Genesis 1:1–3). This is what the Psalmist tells us when he sings: *By the word of God the universe was formed; all that is comes from the breath of God's mouth… For God spoke and reality came to be,* (Psalm 33:6, 9). And this is what the poet of John's Prologue reminds us when he writes: *In the beginning was the Word, and the Word was with God, and the Word was God* (John 1:1).

In the Talmud, the anthology of classical rabbinic law and lore, we learn that every Friday afternoon in preparation for the Sabbath, Rabbis Hanina and Hoshiah would create a "delicious calf" by combining the Hebrew letters for "calf" according to the secrets revealed in *Sefer Yetzirah*, the more-than-ancient Book of Formation (Sanhedrin 65b, 67b). Abraham, so we are told, used the same method from the same book to create the calf he served to the angels who came to tell him of Sarah's coming pregnancy (Genesis 18:7).

This was possible because, as *Sefer Yetzirah* itself makes clear, God formed the letters of the Hebrew *Aleph Beit* as the building blocks of creation. The *Aleph Beit* in Judaism is the equivalent of quanta in physics and DNA in biology. It is through the twenty-two letters of the *Aleph Beit* that God created all reality: everything that was, is, and will ever be. Abraham, Hanina, and Hoshiah knew how to combine these building blocks to make dinner. Theoretically you and I can do the same.

Personally, though, I'd rather order my food from a menu at a fine restaurant than conjure it from the *Aleph Beit* and *Sefer Yetzirah*, but that doesn't mean knowing the mystical depths of the Hebrew letters is of no use to me. On the contrary, while I have an abundance of food, I do not have an abundance of wisdom, and this—rather than dinner—is the greater gift of the *Aleph Beit*. And because it is the greater gift, Richard Seidman's wonderful book, *A New Oracle of Kabbalah: Mystical Teachings of the Hebrew Letters*, is so important. It is, quite simply, a twenty-first century *Sefer Yetzirah*; not a modern translation of the ancient original, but a fresh and contemporary exploration of much of the same material, an exploration of the Hebrew *Aleph Beit* designed not for Jewish mystics alone, but for Wisdomseekers of any faith and none.

If your goal is to serve veal for Friday night dinner by conjuring with the letters *ayin*, *gimmel*, and *lamed* (*egel*, the Hebrew word for *calf*), or to bypass the long years it takes to earn a doctorate in physics or biology by mastering the twenty-two letters of the Hebrew *Aleph Beit* to uncover the secrets of the Big Bang and Before, you are going to be very disappointed in Seidman's book. *A New Oracle of Kabbalah: Mystical Teachings of the Hebrew Letters* isn't for dining or doctorates. It's for diving into the Wisdom that was at the beginning; the Wisdom that was with God; the Wisdom that is God.

A New Oracle of Kabbalah is a welcoming doorway into the transformative power of the Hebrew *Aleph Beit*. Mr. Seidman's insights into the letters, and Shoshannah Brombacher's artistic rendering of the letters in the accompanying card deck, bring the genius and beauty of the *Aleph Beit* to anyone who desires it. Together they invite you into an interior world of silence and primal sound out of which the universe grows like a rose on a rose bush. But, as with the rose, there is both beauty and thorn.

The beauty—both philosophical and artistic—I will let you discover on your own. Read the book; meditate on the cards; you will see what you can; and as your gaze softens your seeing sharpens and you will come to know even more. But regarding the thorns, let me offer this caveat: the *Aleph Beit* is more poetry than prose.

In Hebrew the words for *word, speech,* and *thing* share a single root: *dalet-beit-resh (d-v-r).* In the Hebrew mind the word and the thing are inextricable. When God said "Light!" light happened. It wasn't that God said "Light!" and *then* light happened. There was no *then,* no lag in time between saying and being. The word, speaking the word, and the object spoken of by that word happened in the same instance. For the Jew, being is happening, and the Divine Being, whose very Name, Y-H-V-H, is a form of the Hebrew verb "to be," is the happening of all, in all, with all, as all. What is so of God, however, is not so of us.

For us there is a link between an object and its name, but not an equivalence. The word *milk* cannot satisfy a baby's thirst. The word *fire* cannot scorch a single twig. This is what Lao Tzu reminds us in the opening of his *Tao Te Ching*: *The tao that can be spelled, the tao that can be spoken, is not the truest Tao* (*Tao Te Ching* 1:1).

While I encourage you to learn the letters of the *Aleph Beit,* I warn you against falling under their spell. It is not an accident that we speak of magic spells . . . spells are spelling . . . combining letters, making words, crafting realities. To fall under their spell is to fall into the trap of literalism: to make magic of a subtler mysticism, and prose of a subtler poetry.

You must always leave room not only for the unsaid, but also the unsayable: the Tao that cannot be spelled or spoken. This is why the first letter of the *Aleph Beit* is silent; reminding you that all that follows is but an echo of the unsaid and unsayable.

This is why Seidman and Brombacher needed to collaborate: the letters speak to the left side of the brain, the pictures to the right, and together they invite a whole-mindedness that can discover the Wisdom as soundless Word. This is why you need to read the book and contemplate the images. I admire *A New Oracle of Kabbalah: Mystical Teachings of the Hebrew Letters* for what it teaches; I recommend it for what it does: opening you to the silent breath quivering over the depths of chaos just before the birth of sound and the happening that is life.

Rabbi Rami Shapiro
Christmas Day 2014

PREFACE TO THE 2015 EDITION

This edition of *Oracle of Kabbalah* is a revised and expanded version of the book that was first published in 2001.

Writing this book was an act of holy *chutzpah* on my part as I am by no means an "expert" in Kabbalah. But I am able to synergize divergent paths and make arcane teachings accessible to many people. Perhaps my "beginner's mind" gives this material a fresh feeling, one that appeals to both Jews and non-Jews, and which has provided inspiration and guidance to many readers since the initial publication.

When the remaining inventory of the first edition, about 4,000 copies, was accidentally destroyed by an error at the publisher's warehouse, the rights to the book reverted to me. I feel that now is the time to bring this body of work back to life, resurrected from the ashes so to speak, to sprout back into the world.

I wrote the original edition between 1997 and 1999. Since 1999, much has changed for me personally and, of course, for the world.

Just three days after the *Oracle*'s original publication, 9/11 took place when the two towers of the World Trade Center in my hometown of New York City were destroyed by terrorists. The book found its way into the world during this time of collective trauma and sorrow, and then during the violent reaction of the misguided war in Iraq, which proved once again Martín Prechtel's point that grief, un-metabolized, inevitably turns to violence.

I remember the people who have passed away during these last fourteen years. There's an African proverb that elders are wise because they know more dead people. By that standard, I have gained in wisdom since the original publication.

My mother, Phoebe Seidman, died in August 2008. My brother and I and our wives were blessed to be with her as she took her last breath. Her final words to me were, "Have a good trip."

A few months later, a friend from early childhood took his own life.

Soon after that, Rabbi Aryeh Hirschfield, the main inspiration for my book and my connection to Jewish mysticism, drowned, leaving hundreds of students and friends and congregants, as well as his family, suddenly bereft.

Even though I wasn't young in the 1990s when I wrote the first edition, when I look back to that period of my life, I seem to myself naive, acting as if I had all the time in the world. Now, with both of my parents dead and my beloved rabbi no longer in this world, and being closer to ninety years old than to thirty, I have a more acute sense of the passage of time and of the strangeness and preciousness of life.

I have also studied more in these past fourteen years. For most of that time, I trained with Paul Richards, a gifted seer, author, and teacher, who deepened my understanding of energetic presence and empowerment and of the energetic realms that exist parallel to the physical and mental ones.

Martín Prechtel's school in New Mexico, Bolad's Kitchen, has been a place of profound investigation into the syndrome of fleeing and diaspora and displacement that has affected all the world's peoples, not only Jews, for thousands of years, and is mirrored by the fleeing of our own natural souls within the landscape of our bodies. The school is a place where we can discover or rediscover the cultural ingenuity that is in our bones, and resides, possibly dormant, in our thumbs and hands.

I have trained diligently in Shotokan Karate for thirteen years with the remarkable Sensei Aaron Ortega Piddington. This practice has helped ground me in the body, providing an important counterweight to getting too "heady."

Stephen Victor has been my guide through the world of "family constellations" and "organizational constellations" based on the teachings of German therapist, Bert Hellinger. This work has helped me experience more directly the "beingness" of all things, including the Hebrew letters.

All of these paths, in addition to the original Jewish, Buddhist, and Native American viewpoints that powered the original edition, inform this new version of *Oracle of Kabbalah* and give it what I feel is a deeper and broader perspective than that of the original book.

In addition, I have been influenced by comments and feedback from users of the *Oracle*. These responses, including stories of how *Oracle of Kabbalah* has changed and enriched their lives, encouraged me to write this new and expanded investigation into the marvelous character and personalities and powers embodied in each of the ancient Hebrew letters.

I feel strongly that the being of this book wants to be in the world. The book wants to be read and pondered and criticized and used by sincere spiritual seekers and explorers. I feel I owe it to the book itself, as well as to the people who read it, to set this volume out into the world, like launching a boat onto the current, hoping for the best as it drifts out toward the vast ocean where the tides of Chance move unpredictably yet inexorably.

May you be enlivened and heartened, amused and inspired by reading *A New Oracle of Kabbalah*. May it contribute to a richer, happier, more soulful life for you and for those with whom you share its teachings. I am honored by your attention to this book, and wish you all blessings.

Richard Seidman,
Ashland, Oregon, USA
July 2015

PREFACE TO THE 2001 EDITION

One Passover in the early 1990s, during a *seder* at my friend Abby Layton's house, I first caught a glimpse of a Judaism that was fresh, vibrant, and spiritually satisfying.

My Jewish education had been deadening. I attended Hebrew school just long enough to learn the bare minimum needed for a *bar mitzvah*. This involved learning how to sound out Hebrew words without knowing what the words meant. Questions I had about God were rebuffed or ignored by the rabbis and teachers. They all seemed tired from their day jobs.

I endured the yelling of the mean-spirited cantor who was my *bar mitzvah* teacher, and sounded my way through the ceremony, grateful that the long ordeal was almost over. Then I was free. I left Judaism behind, feeling that it was a lifeless, arrogant, and hypocritical path. Later, I added "sexist" and "anthropocentric" to my list of criticisms.

Spiritual yearnings and aspirations soon arose, however. Shortly after college, I became a serious student of Zen Buddhism, and then, for several years, of Christian Science, before returning to the practice of Zen. I began participating in traditional Native American sweat lodges and other Indian ceremonies. I studied the mythopoetic teachings of Joseph Campbell, Robert Bly, Michael Meade, and others. For more than twenty years, religious practices of various forms, but not Jewish practices, were at the center of my life.

Even though both my mother's parents had grown up in Medzibozh, Ukraine, the home of the great mystic, the Baal Shem Tov, and the location of many magical stories about the Baal Shem and his disciples, I remained ignorant of any forms of Judaism other than the sterile Reform and Conservative temples of my youth and the fundamentalist Orthodox ones shown on the news.

The *seder* at Abby's house was an eye-opener. Could Judaism actually be joyful, ecstatic, profound, practical, earth-based, and non-sexist? A couple of years later, I read Rodger Kamenetz's book, *The Jew in the*

Lotus. Here was more evidence of a vital and dynamic Judaism, along with portraits of others who blended Buddhist and Jewish ways.

Around that time, a medicine man named Martín Prechtel performed a divination ceremony for me. He recommended that I learn some Hebrew. He said that my ancestors had been consumed by a great fire and that part of my destiny was to help bring their lost voices back to life.

Through Abby, I met Rabbi Aryeh Hirschfield. A student of the influential teachers Rabbi Shlomo Carlebach and Rabbi Zalman Schachter-Shalomi, Aryeh was proof that an enlightened, humane, humorous, and deeply spiritual Judaism is possible. I started attending the Jewish Renewal services he led in Portland, Oregon.

Gradually, I began to see how the various spiritual paths I had followed resonated with one another. For me, it was no longer a question of Judaism versus Buddhism versus indigenous practices. Each had its own integrity, and each spoke to me in different ways. Judaism was the religion of my ancestors, however, and it felt important to be reconnected with this deep part of my heritage.

In 1997, I became intrigued by folklore and mystical teachings regarding the Hebrew alphabet. As I learned more, many of my long-term interests found a focus in the *Aleph Beit*. For each letter is an archetype and each letter is a *koan* and each letter is a dream and each letter is a poem.

I began studying the *Aleph Beit* in earnest. As I did so, the letters came alive for me. I gained an appreciation for the subtlety and profundity of the Hebrew language. Familiar words such as *shalom* or *mayim* took on deeper significance as I became more intimate with their component letters. As dreams or archetypes or poems, the letters, I realized, could serve as guides or teachers, initiating one into deeper levels of intuition and spiritual understanding. I read how Abraham Abulafia and other Jewish mystics would meditate upon the letters and use them in just such a fashion.

The letters retain their ancient, archetypal power, and yet I found most of the contemporary books on the *Aleph Beit* written in English at the time to be arcane and confusing and very dry.

I also felt frustrated that almost all of the sources I studied approached Jewish spirituality from a narrowly Jewish point of view. It was as if Shakespeare, Yeats, Bashō, Kabir, Rumi, and the rest of "non-Jewish" culture, not to mention other religions and indigenous peoples, had nothing worthwhile to share when it came to Jewish mysticism.

I decided to write *Oracle of Kabbalah* with the intention that the traditional teachings regarding the letters would be presented in an enjoyable and clear, practical way, one that would be accessible to readers no matter their level of Jewish knowledge or sophistication, or whether or not they considered themselves Jewish. This revised edition expands upon the earlier book.

The perspectives gleaned during three and a half decades of meditation, study, prayer, and exploration inform this book. *A New Oracle of Kabbalah* borrows from other traditions to amplify or clarify its themes, but remains grounded in traditional and mystical Judaism. At the same time, I incorporate writings and teachings from a variety of religious and cultural paths to provide perspective on the materials. The result, I hope, is one that is deeply Jewish but not narrowly so.

As I began to consult this oracle for guidance and insight, and help friends do so as well, the letters spoke to us with clarity.

For example, when one friend, despite doubts and confusion, was about to move across the country, she selected *Beit*, the sign of house and blessing. The message was clear: she could aspire to find an inner sense of home to ground her even as she journeyed to and fro. She could hallow the place where she found herself instead of always looking for someplace better. Also, she could maintain an intention to be a blessing to those she encountered in the course of her travels.

A woman confronting a life-threatening illness chose *Gimmel*. This sign of the camel reassured her that, like a camel, she possessed the resources she needed to make it through her frightening "desert" experience. Inspired by *Gimmel*'s counsel to perform deeds of loving-kindness, this woman, instead of getting stuck in a sinkhole of self-pity, rededicated herself to extending love to those she encountered.

Another friend was anxious about enrolling in a week-long dance and tai chi workshop. Well into his fifties and very shy, he had never done much dancing. This class was an attempt to break through to a new, freer way of moving, but he was nervous. Was he too old, too stiff, too awkward? The letter he selected, *Chet*, encouraged him to have holy *chutzpah*, to confront his fear and move through the gate of transition into a new level of experience.

In the thirteenth century, Abraham Abulafia wrote of the *Aleph Beit*, "Every letter represents a whole world to the mystic who abandons himself [or herself] to its contemplation."[1]

I hope that, like generations of people before us, as you abandon yourself, you find exploring these worlds to be helpful, inspiring, and joyful.

INTRODUCTION

The Letters of Creation

The Hebrew word for "letter," אות — *ot* — also means "sign" or "wonder" or "miracle." For thousands of years, Jewish sages have taught that the letters of the Hebrew alphabet, the *Aleph Beit*, embody wonderful and miraculous powers.

According to the earliest known book on Jewish mysticism, *The Sefer Yetzirah* (*The Book of Creation*), written more than fifteen centuries ago, God formed the entire universe through speaking aloud the twenty-two letters. With the vibration of God's cosmic utterances, out of the nothingness of silence all things spring to life. "God said, 'Let there be light.' And there was light."

The letters of the *Aleph Beit*, as the manifestations of God's voice, are the energetic and vibrational building blocks of creation. They are analogous to physical elements. Just as, for example, an atom of oxygen gas unites with two atoms of hydrogen gas to form a molecule of water, so does one letter combine with another to create new beings.

Rabbi Marcia Prager writes, "This perception of Hebrew words and letters as the constituent spiritual elements of existence undergirds most Jewish mystical teaching."[1]

The letters are archetypes. Each one expresses a specific primordial power or creative energy. For example, ב, *Beit*, is the sign of "house." מ, *Mem*, is the letter of water and the womb. David Abram puts it this way: "Each letter of the *Aleph Beit* is assumed by the Kabbalists to have its own personality, its own profound magic, its own way of organizing the whole of existence around itself."[2]

The thirteenth-century masterpiece of Jewish mysticism, *The Zohar, The Book of Splendor*, says, "For when the world was created, it was the supernal letters that brought into being all the works of the lower world, literally after their pattern. Hence, whoever has a knowledge of them and is observant of them is beloved both on high and below."[3]

Unlike Indo-European languages, in Hebrew, each letter also is a number. The characters do double duty, serving simultaneously as numerals and as sounds.

The Hebrew letters, therefore, represent not just the sound of creation but also the *mathematics* of creation. We are all numerals in the vast equation of the universe that is at the same time the song, the musical score, of the universe. (The word "score" suggests the mathematical basis of music.) All life is created by the infinite combinations of holy numbers that are also letters of the *Aleph Beit*.

For centuries, Jewish mystics and scholars have cultivated knowledge and observance of the *Aleph Beit*, and a vast folklore and mystical tradition arose regarding the letters. In the thirteenth century, Abraham Abulafia developed practices for meditating on the letters that make up God's numerous holy names. He taught how to permutate and combine these letters to elicit heightened spiritual states.

Abulafia and other Kabbalists created elaborate theories regarding the role of each letter, its numerical force, and its special place in creation and in forming the words of the Torah.

They believed in the power of the Hebrew letters to affect reality in profound ways. For example, some rabbis and students invoked spells in attempts to create *golems*, human-like creatures made of clay. The word "spell" indicates the magical powers inherent in the combining of letters. One well-known spell, the incantational phrase "abracadabra," may stem from the Hebrew *abra k'adabra*, which literally means, "I will create as I speak."

The power of the letters to manifest as physical objects is reflected in the shared root of the Hebrew words for "word" and "thing," דבור, *dibur*, and דבר, *davar*. Words are things, and things are words made manifest.

In the Torah, the Ten Commandments are not referred to as "Commandments," but rather *Aseret ha'Dibrot*, "the Ten Utterances" or "the Ten Sayings." *The Zohar* describes how God's speech created the tablets bearing these Ten Utterances: "When these letters came forth, they were all refined, carved precisely, sparkling, flashing. All of Israel saw the letters flying through space in every direction, engraving themselves on the tablets of stone."[4]

In the eighteenth century, the movement called Hasidism arose in Eastern Europe. It was led by Israel ben Eliezer, known as the Baal Shem Tov or Master of the Good Name. There had existed other Baal Shems or Masters of the Name before Israel ben Eliezer. The title alludes to mastery of the ability to combine and permutate the letters of God's holy name for the purposes of healing and blessing. The Baal Shem Tov taught a joyful, accessible form of mysticism. Rejecting the legalistic approach of traditional rabbinical Judaism, the Baal Shem Tov and his followers emphasized the power of simple, heartfelt prayer. This attitude is reflected in teaching stories regarding the *Aleph Beit*.

In one of them, a poor Jewish farmer was riding his horse into town to pray at the synagogue for *Yom Kippur*. But a heavy fog settled on the countryside and he could not find his way. As darkness fell, he was lost in a forest and was going to spend *Yom Kippur* night there by himself.

This farmer didn't have a prayer book. And he didn't know the prayers by heart. Filled with anguish, he cried out, "Oh, God, what can I do? How can I pray to You?" Then he remembered the alphabet he had learned in his childhood. He said, "I know. I will recite the letters of the *Aleph Beit* and You, Holy One, You know all the words, You can put the letters together to form the right prayers for *Yom Kippur*." So, all that night he repeated the letters over and over.

When the Baal Shem Tov heard about this, he said that not only was this humble prayer pleasing to the Holy One, but its power was so great that many people, even those more learned, had their prayers accepted that *Yom Kippur* because of the sincerity and purity of this simple farmer's *Aleph Beit*.

The attitude that each letter of the *Aleph Beit* is sacred is shown in the way a Torah scroll is created. Every Torah is handwritten. Not a single letter can be missing, erased or smudged, nor may any letter touch another. If so, the whole scroll is considered invalid.

Jiri Langer writes in *Nine Gates to the Hasidic Mysteries*, "When a book is so badly torn that it cannot be used, the caretaker takes it to the cemetery and buries it. Even the smallest scrap of paper with Hebrew characters printed on it must not be left lying about on the floor, or trodden on; it must be buried. For every Hebrew letter is a name of God."[5]

For centuries, Jewish mystics, and some Christian ones, too, have turned to these "names of God" for guidance and inspiration. For centuries, people have meditated upon the letters and reflected on their special powers. By trying to become more intimate with the building blocks of creation, these spiritual seekers hoped to become more intimate with the Creator. The Baal Shem Tov taught, "Enter into every letter with all your strength. God dwells in each letter and as you enter it, you become one with God."[6]

Inspiring the Language: Breath and the Absence of Vowels in Ancient Hebrew

The Hebrew letters represent consonant sounds only. The vowels are filled in by the breath of the reader. In modern Hebrew, vowels are indicated by symbols inserted above, below, or beside the consonants.

Reading ancient Hebrew is thus a profoundly interactive experience. The language comes fully alive only when spoken aloud. David Abram writes, "The Hebrew letters and texts were not sufficient unto themselves; in order to be read, they had to be added to, enspirited by the reader's breath."[7]

Not only does the reader inspire the text through his or her breath, the absence of written vowels compels the reader to actively engage with the text to decide which vowels to choose to insert. Abram continues, "There was no single, definitive meaning; the ambiguity entailed by the lack of written vowels ensured that diverse readings, diverse shades of meaning, were always possible."[8]

Despite — or because of — this ambiguity, ancient Hebrew retains a powerful eloquence. In the introduction to his translation of Genesis, Stephen Mitchell writes, "[Ancient Hebrew's] dignity comes from its supreme simplicity. It is a language of concision and powerful earthiness, austere in its vocabulary, straightforward in its syntax, spare with its adjectives and adverbs — a language that pulses with the energy of elemental human truths."[9]

Divination in Judaism: Abomination or Source of Guidance?

Divination has been viewed ambivalently throughout Jewish history. On the one hand, there is the strong injunction in Deuteronomy: "Among you, there shall not be found anyone who passes his son or daughter through fire, who practices stick divination, who divines auspicious times, who divines by omens, who practices witchcraft, who uses incantations, who consults mediums and oracles, or who attempts to communicate with the dead. Anyone involved in these practices is repulsive to God, and it was because of repulsive practices such as these that God your Lord is driving out [these nations] before you. You must [therefore] remain totally faithful to God your Lord."[10]

On the other hand, Jewish people have continuously practiced various forms of divination. In the days of the Temple, the high priest consulted the *Urim* and *Thummim*, the oracular "breastplate of judgment."[11] After the fall of the Temple, the *Urim* and *Thummim* were lost, but many other divinatory practices remained popular among the common people.

Rabbis from Talmudic times onwards, acknowledging this abiding, ancient, and widespread human tendency, and trying to reconcile it with the decree from Deuteronomy, developed a distinction between "divination" and "signs." They considered it improper to try to foretell or influence the future through magical means, which they labeled "divination," but acceptable to attempt to deepen one's understanding or ask for divine guidance from "signs." In many cases, this distinction was more semantic than practical. The *Encyclopaedia Judaica* reports, "The distinction between divination and signs is sometimes so fine as to be almost imperceptible."[12]

The Hebrew word for "letter" also means "sign" and, for hundreds of years, Jewish mystics have consulted the signs of the *Aleph Beit* as a means to deepen insight. Abraham Abulafia, for example, wrote in the thirteenth century that "the letters are without question the root of all wisdom and knowledge, and they themselves are the substance of prophecy. In a prophetic vision, they appear as if they were solid bodies, actually speaking to the individual."[13]

A New Oracle of Kabbalah and Divination

A New Oracle of Kabbalah can serve as an oracle and a means of divination. One definition of "oracle" is "an authoritative or wise expression or answer." It comes from the Latin word meaning "to speak." It is appropriate that these letters "speak" to us as they are the written representatives of human speech, and in Jewish thought, they are also the agents by which God's speech calls all things into being. Listening to the oracle of these letters, therefore, can be an entryway into hearing the word, the song, of Creation.

There are two basic definitions of the word "divination." The first is: "the art or practice that seeks to foresee or foretell future events or discover hidden knowledge, usually by means of augury or by the aid of supernatural powers." The second meaning of divination is "unusual insight or intuitive perception." This latter definition is the one intended with respect to *A New Oracle of Kabbalah*.

The letters, in other words, don't foretell future events and don't rely on supernatural powers. They will, however, show considerations to keep in mind as you weigh possible courses of action. Allow the letters to activate your insight and intuitive perception, and they will serve as a kind of divining rod, leading you to currents of thought and life lying below the surface of things. "Look at these holy letters with truth and belief," Abraham Abulafia wrote seven hundred years ago, "[it] will awaken the heart to thoughts of godly and prophetic images."[14]

A New Oracle of Kabbalah makes some of the power of the Hebrew letters accessible and practical to contemporary people. The book can be a valuable and enjoyable way for modern readers to enter into the profound world of these letters. Knowledge of Hebrew is not necessary. The main requirements are a curious mind, a receptive heart, and a playful, even childlike, spirit.

A New Oracle of Kabbalah represents merely an introduction into the depths of the Hebrew alphabet. Many other books explore the subject much more completely. Please see the bibliography for suggestions for more in-depth study.

The Art of Consulting
A New Oracle of Kabbalah

To use the letters as a means of divination, buy or create your own deck of Hebrew letter cards. (See page xi.) Then, formulate your question, choose one or more cards depending on the kind of "spread" you are using, and see the potential paths and lessons to be learned that the letter reveals. As mentioned above, אות, *ot*, the word for "letter" in Hebrew (which begins with the first letter of the *Aleph Beit* and ends with the last) also means "sign" or "symbol" or "miracle."

The Book of Isaiah says, "Ask for a letter [a sign] of the Holy One. Ask it either in the depth below or in the height above."[15] The intention, or *kavanah*, you have in asking is crucial. As you uplift or deepen your *kavanah*, the response of the cards will touch you that much more highly or deeply.

I have noticed that when one consults the *Oracle* in a frivolous way, without thinking of a heartfelt question beforehand and without approaching the letters respectfully and prayerfully, the results seem less relevant or clear.

The basic way to use the *Oracle* is to become quiet for a few minutes and enter into a receptive, meditative attitude. Take three slow, deep breaths from the belly. Formulate a question for which you seek the guidance of the *Aleph Beit*. Avoid "yes" or "no" questions. A good generic question is, "What perspective on this matter can the letters provide?"[16] Pray for inspiration and receptivity.

Once you've taken sufficient time to formulate an earnest inquiry, keeping your question in mind, shuffle the cards and spread them face down on a table or in your hand.

In helping people use the *Oracle* for divination and self-discovery, I have observed that often there is a question beneath the original question. The response of the letters can help uncover that deeper question. Sometimes the response of the *Oracle* doesn't seem to be relevant to the initial question. When that happens, see if there is a more fundamental question underlying the original one, and whether the letters that are chosen address that more profound question.

Some good times to consult the *Aleph Beit* include:

- upon first waking up in the morning — to set a theme for the coming day.

- after a period of prayer or meditation — to see what additional insights emerge from a place of inner quiet and receptivity.

- at sunrise or sunset — to mark the turnings of the day.

- at the time of Rosh Chodesh, the new moon — to set a theme for the coming month.

- on Shabbos — to focus one's prayers during this day of rest and renewal.

- at Havdalah, the ceremony marking the end of Shabbos and the beginning of the new week — to set a theme for the coming week.

- before going to sleep — to welcome the archetypal power of the letters to enter one's dreams.

- before embarking on a journey — to be aware of opportunities for spiritual growth while one is away from home.

Early Kabbalist practitioners reported that after periods of meditating upon the alphabet, the letters came to life and began talking. Others said they saw the letters grow wings and fly from the surface of the page.[17] Even if your experience is less dramatic, perhaps the letters will speak quietly to you.

For those who know Hebrew, the cards can be combined to form words. New insights may be gleaned regarding these words as we see more deeply into the significance of the component letters. The traditional numerical values of each letter are indicated for those with an interest in *Gematria*, the calculation of the numerical value of Hebrew words and the search for connections with other words or phrases of equal value.

Each chapter begins with a description of the basic meanings associated with that chapter's letter. It then suggests various ways the energies of the letter might apply to one's life or inform one's question. Shadow, or problematic, aspects of the letter are then discussed. Personal comments of the author come next, followed by a chapter summary.

At the end of the summary is a suggested action, a kind of *mitzvah* for that particular letter. *Mitzvah* is usually translated as "commandment" or "good deed." Its root, though, is "connection." These suggested actions are examples of ways to connect tangibly and practically with the power of each letter. They are certainly not commandments, although in some cases they might inspire good deeds.

Types of Readings and "Spreads"

One-Card Reading: Single Letter, Many Paths

The simplest method is to select one card, and discover what sign is revealed to you. Look up the description of that letter in the text and see how the ideas there correspond with or illumine your situation or question. Meditate upon the letter's associations and also the emotional tone it evokes within you.

Abraham Abulafia advised students to concentrate on the letters "in all their aspects, like a person who is told a parable, or a riddle, or a dream, or as one who ponders a book of wisdom in a subject so profound. . ."[18] Ponder the answer to your question as you would a riddle or a dream.

In your imagination, *become* the letter. You are not just someone who "chose," for example, the letter *Dalet*, which means "door," you are the door itself, opening up. You are not just a human who happened to pick *Gimmel*, the symbol of the camel, you are the camel, making your way steadily through a desert. You are not just a person who is reading about *Nun*, the energy of "fish," you are the fish itself, swimming through the ever-changing waters of life. Experience the cards in this way and they will speak to you more intimately. As Rabbi Abraham Joshua Heschel has written, "The ultimate way is not to have a symbol but to be a symbol, to stand for the divine."[19]

Another way to use the cards is to select one and then meditate upon it, carefully tracing its shape in your mind's eye and seeing what thoughts, images, feelings, or inspirations come. After doing this, you may choose to refer to the text to see how the ideas there correspond with your own discoveries, or you may simply be content with the fruits of your own meditation.

Multi-Card Spreads

In addition to the single card method of selecting just one card and pondering the layers of interpretation it offers, you can also create "spreads" by choosing more than one card at a time.

Spreads have the potential to provide a fuller, more multi-dimensional response to your inquiry. They also have the potential to become confusing or overwhelming. I encourage you to experiment with spreads only after you are well familiar with the basic meanings and associations of each letter.

Then, when you are interpreting the results of your spread, you need not read the entire chapter for each letter, but can merely review the chapter summary to get the basic sense of the Oracle's response, and how the various letters of the spreads relate to each other and respond to your question.

Two-Card Spread: Sacred Marriage

For this spread, choose one card to represent "masculine," *Yang*, direct-action energy. Place it on your right.

Choose a second card to represent "feminine," *Yin*, indirect-action energy. Place this card on your left.

The letter of the right hand indicates specific actions that can be helpful in addressing the question you have brought to the spread. What "masculine" qualities would be good for you to internalize and bring into play in the current situation? This letter will help reveal the qualities that lend themselves to direct action.

The letter of the left hand indicates some specific ways that the subtle, receptive power of the feminine's great abilities of indirect, spirally action can shed light on your question.

Between these two cards, a force field can emerge. This is the "third thing" of the marriage of the masculine and the feminine. As you experience this inner marriage of your male side and your female side as illustrated through the combination of these two letters, perhaps you will receive an inspiration or perspective on your situation that is not wholly revealed by just one side or the other.

It takes the synergy of the two sides to create a whole that is greater than the sum of the parts. What is the new direction revealed to you through this marriage? What new possibilities might be birthed into the world through their combination?

Three-Card Spread: Past, Present, Future

Prepare for selecting the cards in the same prayerful and contemplative way you do when selecting a single card.

When you are ready, choose an initial letter to represent elements of the past that are influencing the current situation. These may be habits or circumstances to let go of and release, or to bow down to and thank, or to grieve for. In all cases, we are called to affirm this sign of the past as being the root of the present moment. The letter may also indicate actions that could be helpful in resolving impediments or unknotting entanglements from the past.

Note which letter had been selected, and put that card back in the deck, shuffle the cards again, and choose a second letter to represent the present situation. Or, if you prefer, keep the first letter on the table and choose from the remaining letters.

The second letter drawn gives perspective on the forces at play right now, providing a spiritual snapshot of the current moment. It may also provide hints for actions and attitudes that will help move the situation forward in a positive direction. It gives you your marching orders.

Replace that card in the deck, shuffle the deck, and choose a third letter, or do not replace it and choose from the remaining letters. The third letter is the letter of the future. It indicates the direction the situation is heading, the kind of actions and attitudes that will be called for in the future.

If you choose to replace the cards after each selection and you wind up choosing the same letter for two or even three of these temporal planes, it reinforces the importance of the lessons of that letter. Pay extra close attention. This could indicate a kind of stasis on one hand, and the need to shake things up, or, on the other hand, a unity of past, present, and future that can be celebrated.

Five-Card Spread: Angels

There is a section of the "Bedtime *Shema*," the prayers uttered before going to sleep, that invokes the protection of four angels and the *Shechinah*, the feminine, in-dwelling aspect of the Divine:

> In the name of Ha-shem, the God of Israel,
> On my right is Michael, on my left is Gabriel
> Before me is Uriel, behind me Raphael
> Above me and all around me, Shekinat-El.

For the Angels Spread, prepare to select the cards in the usual, deep, contemplative and prayerful way. *Malach*, the Hebrew word for "angel," means "messenger." What messages do each of these angels have for us?

You can place the selected cards in front of you similar to the other spreads, or, better yet, you can place the cards around your body according to the following directions.

Choose the first card to represent the message of Michael. The name "Michael" means "Who is like God?" or more literally, "Who is like Force?" He is the angel of kindness and expansiveness. Place this card toward your right.

The next letter represents the message of Gabriel, the angel of strength and creating clear borders and boundaries. Gabriel's name means "Strength of God" or "Strong Force." Place this card to your left.

The third letter represents the message of Uriel, the angel of light, of vision, inspiration, and of what is dawning. Uriel's name means "Light of God" or "Light Force." Place this card directly in front of you, forward of the others.

The fourth letter represents the message of Raphael, the angel of healing. This angel's name means "Healing of God" or "Healing Force." Place this card in the center and beneath the others.

The fifth and final letter represents the message of *Shechinah*, the feminine presence of the Holy, the way that heaven's energy has come down into your body and is moving in your body and your life right now. Place this card right in the middle of all the others, or hold it overhead or even directly under you.

One way to interpret the Angels Spread is to assume that each letter is the voice of that particular angel or the *Shechinah*. It is sending you a message, and also singing to you a song of protection. The energies of that letter are communicating to you and watching over you.

The angels might also be showing you areas of your life to cultivate to become more like them. In other words, the letter you select for Michael may point toward ways you can become even more kind and loving within the context of the question or situation you have brought to the *Oracle*.

The letter for Gabriel might indicate the path for you to take to deepen your expressions of strength and discernment vis-à-vis this situation.

The letter for Uriel could hint at ways of bringing greater vision and enlightenment into your life. This angel leads the way. It represents the sunrise in the east, the dawning of a new day.

The letter for Raphael describes the context of healing, and suggests ways for you to bring healing to the question or matter you are contemplating.

Finally, the letter of the *Shechinah* indicates fundamental circumstances that are at the very heart of your life and the current situation. You are inundated in the energies of this letter. It is above you, below you, inside you, and all around you. This card is a call to open your heart and take in the spirit and power the letter offers. It will bring transformation.

Have Fun

Whether you are choosing several cards for a spread or just a single card for a basic reading, I encourage you to have fun with these letters. Approach them respectfully, but with a spirit of play, and they will be your friends. May the letters of the *Aleph Beit* stimulate your mind. May they provide guidance and direction to your actions and speech. May they blaze through your heart like the sound of a *shofar*. May they help you feel closer to the Great Mystery and to all beings.

CHAPTER ONE

Aleph

(ah'leph)

SOUND: silent[1]

NUMERICAL VALUE: 1; 1,000; numberless

Meanings

Aleph and *aluph*, Hebrew for "leader" or "chieftain," share the same root, אלף. *Aleph*, the first letter of the *Aleph Beit*, is the chief of all the letters that follow it.

In the Hebrew numerical system, where each letter represents a number, *Aleph* equals the number one. It is also the first letter of the word for "one," אחד, *echad*. *Aleph* symbolizes the central teaching of Judaism, that God is one.

Aleph is the first letter of the first word of the Ten Utterances (a.k.a. the Ten Commandments), אנכי, *anoki*, "I." All the 613 commandments of the Torah follow the lead of this chief. All the commandments trace their essence to *Aleph*, the symbol of the Holy One.

At the same time, however, *Aleph* shares the same root as *eleph*, Hebrew for the number one thousand. This denotes both the specific numeral 1,000 and also a vastly large, innumerable quantity. *Aleph*, embodying both unity and multiplicity, is thus the prime factor

15

of creation, leading the other letters as they combine to form the phenomena of the universe.

Computers are driven by an either/or, yes/no model of reality, and all of modern life seems more and more infused with this simplistic and reductionistic viewpoint.

Aleph slips the clutches of the limitations of "computer mind," of simplistic dichotomies, of narrow labeling and pigeonholing, and black-and-white thinking.

This letter of simultaneous oneness and numberlessness begins several names of God including *Elohim*, אלהים, and *Adonai*, אדני.

Interestingly, the name *Elohim* is a plural word that literally means "Forces." God is at the same time one and many and beyond all such distinctions.

Another name for God is *Ein Sof*, literally "Without End." Ein Sof is related to the word אין, *ayin*, which begins with an *Aleph* and means "nothing." Aryeh Kaplan explains that the term *Ein Sof* has the connotation of "the Ultimate Nothingness."[2] The essence of *Aleph* and of our lives is, paradoxically, nothingness.

Aleph's essence of nothingness is reflected in its sound. It has none. The very first letter of the *Aleph Beit* is silent! *Aleph* is the sound that comes before sound. *Aleph* is so close to the divine essence, on the edge of the holy nothingness from which sound and form emerge, that it can't be constrained within a particular sound. We "pronounce" *Aleph* by opening our mouths but saying nothing, as if we were speechless with awe and wonder.

Aleph coalesces into form that which is formless. It makes solid that which cannot be grasped. At the same time, *Aleph* retains the pre-alphabetic condition, when "the earth was without form, and empty."[3]

Out of this emptiness, experience flashes vividly into being. God says, "Let there be light" and there is light. Earth, air, water, and fire come into form. Three of these four elements begin with *Aleph*: אדמה, *adamah*, "earth"; אויר, *avir*, "air"; and אש, *esh*, "fire."

Application

When *Aleph* materializes in our hands, it is an opportunity to recall what is primary. *Aleph* indicates a time to strip away the superfluous and get back to basics, to essentials, to what is elemental in our existence. What are our priorities? Where, given the vastness of the universe, amid the swirlings of numerous intents, will we focus our energies?

Aleph is a transcendental letter that is at the same time at home in the elements. When selecting *Aleph*, we have a big challenge: to be grounded in the earth, air, and fire of daily life while staying aware of the cosmic emptiness of *ayin*, nothingness.

"Rabbi Aaron of Karlin was asked what he had learned from his teacher, the Great Maggid. 'Nothing at all,' he said. And when they pressed him to explain what he meant by that, he added: 'The nothing-at-all is what I learned. I learned the meaning of nothingness. I learned that I am nothing at all, and that I Am, notwithstanding.'"[4]

The basic ambiguity of existence Rabbi Aaron is describing is expressed through *Aleph*. The word "ambiguity" has an original meaning of "driving in two directions." *Aleph* drives two ways: toward oneness and toward numberlessness, toward nothingness and toward "I Amness." The Buddhist "Heart of Perfect Wisdom Sutra" describes this same dynamic: "Form is exactly emptiness, emptiness exactly form."

Aleph challenges us to live, at least for a little while, without being constrained within an "either/or" mindset.

Rabbi Yerachmiel Ben Yisrael put it this way: "God must be both *Yesh* and *Ayin*, Being and Emptiness, simultaneously. *Yesh* and *Ayin* reside in and are expressions of God's wholeness (*shlemut*)."[5]

How can we simultaneously embrace form and emptiness, something and nothing? How can we truly feel the oneness of creation within the infinite variety of its forms? Reb Yerachmiel wrote, "The purpose of Judaism is not other than the purpose of any authentic religion: the unification of *Yesh* and *Ayin*, Being and Emptiness, in the awakened consciousness of humankind."[6] How do we discover the unity of such apparently conflicting forces?

The shape of the letter *Aleph* provides some clues. Jewish sages teach that *Aleph* represents: (1) the yoke of an ox, (2) the upper and lower waters separated by the sky, and (3) a ladder. Each of these images can give us some guidance in making peace with the ambiguity of *Aleph*, the ambiguity of our lives.

In addition to *Aleph*'s shape resembling the yoke of an ox (especially in its earlier historic Phoenician form), the word *Aleph* is related to a Hebrew word for "ox," *aluph*. An ox is an animal of tremendous power and fortitude. When this power is tamed and harnessed, it helps people cultivate fields and provide the food of life. "A rich harvest comes through the strength of the ox."[7] The ox represents the spiritual power we have within us. The yoke symbolizes the discipline that contains this incredible ox energy and directs it in positive, nourishing ways.

The central prayer of Judaism is the *Shema*, "Hear O Israel, Y-H-V-H is our God, Y-H-V-H is One."[8] To know this unity beyond duality, we need first to have a *kavanah* or intention to do so. Then, we need the yoke of a spiritual practice that will help us prepare the soil of our minds and souls to directly experience this oneness. This yoke may take the form of daily prayer, meditation, mindful movement, or study. *Aleph* encourages us to take on at least one of these yokes, and to start plowing.

The great Rabbi Isaac Luria taught that the shape of *Aleph*, embodying the ambiguity of driving two ways, had another kind of significance. *Aleph* is formed by the letter *Yud* in the upper right and a *Yud* in the lower left, with the letter *Vav* lying diagonally between them. In Genesis, God says, "There shall be a sky in the middle of the water, and it shall divide between water and water."[9]

According to Rabbi Luria, the upper *Yud* stands for the higher waters, which symbolize the joys of feeling close to God. The lower *Yud* represents the lower waters, which symbolize the bitterness and sorrow of feeling far from God. The *Vav* in the middle simultaneously separates these two waters and connects them.

Aleph is thus a Jewish version of the yin-yang symbol, the Chinese symbol of complementary tendencies. *Aleph* embraces the ambiguity and the balance of form and emptiness, separateness and unity, one-ness and "thousandness." *The Zohar* describes this situation: "Crying is enwedged in my heart on one side, while joy is enwedged in my heart on the other side."[10]

Aleph teaches us to embrace both sides of life, the grief and the joy, the bitter and the sweet, in order to experience the integrity, the undivided completeness of our lives.

The shape of *Aleph* represents a ladder, ascending up to the left. Jacob dreamed of a ladder, set upon the earth and reaching all the way to heaven, upon which the angels of God ascended and descended.[11] *Aleph* is the connector, the bridge, that makes it possible for angels, bearers of divine messages, to flow freely back and forth between the heavenly and the earthly, the world of infinite emptiness and the world of unique form, the numberless and the one.

As we identify as *Aleph*, we become the ox steadfastly plowing the field, preparing the ground for new growth. We become the sky and the waters, simultaneously divided and united. And we become the ladder making the connection between heaven and earth, providing the channel for angels to ascend and descend, opening the way for communication with the Holy.

Then, we can say, as Jacob cried when he awoke from his dream of the ladder, "God truly is in this place but I did not know it...How awe-inspiring this place is! It must be God's temple. It is the gate to heaven!"[12]

Aleph's Shadow

A danger of *Aleph* is to become paralyzed with ambivalence. When we are able to see both sides, we may become like Hamlet, unable to choose and act. We may need to rouse ourselves into action, while recognizing that "not choosing" is itself a choice.

Because *Aleph* is so close to the *Ein Sof*, the Ultimate Nothingness, it carries the danger of leading into nihilism, the belief that existence is senseless and useless. If we have drifted to this extreme, we can recall the other direction *Aleph* moves, toward form and fulfillment.

Aleph drives both ways. We can be alert to the tendency to get stuck in one side or the other of form and emptiness.

Personal Comments

Aleph is hard to grasp. How do we get hold of a letter that has no sound? It's like trying to catch the wind in a butterfly net. Better not to try, I think, and just enjoy the breeze.

Aleph comes from two directions and then — wham! — here we are right at the crux. When I look at *Aleph*, I think of all the mothers and grandmothers and their mothers and grandmothers all the way back through time. I hear their cries as they give birth. I think of all the fathers all the way back. I feel their anxieties and confusions. How precariously these ancestors engendered life and then nursed it along until mysteriously and wonderfully these children grew up and had babies of their own. For generations upon generations this happened, long before hospitals and anesthesia. Amazing! And then it comes down to me, to you. All these couplings, all these birth pains, all the work they did, all the food they ate, the lusts and the loves of these old ones, led to my birth, to your birth. Here we are!

Aleph reminds me of all this, of the beginnings, of the matings, of birth, of promise. *Aleph* births the *Aleph Beit*. It births the Ten Utterances. Its two small lines connect with the bold diagonal line, the connection, the crux in the middle. That's where we are right now, smack in the middle. *Aleph* is basic, fundamental, ancient. *Aleph* is like a rock; it has seen it all.

Summary for Aleph

Numerical value:	1; 1,000; numberless
Meanings:	Chieftain. Oneness and multiplicity. Ambiguity. Ox. Elemental forces.
Application:	Focus our energies on what is elemental and basic.
	Live, at least for a little while, without being constrained within an "either / or" mindset.
	Open ourselves to both the grief and the joy of life.
	Accept the yoke of a spiritual practice.
Shadow:	Ambivalence.
	Nihilism.
Reflection:	What are my priorities? Where, given the vastness of the universe, will I focus my energies?
Suggested action:	Close your eyes. As you open them, imagine you have just been born and are seeing, hearing, smelling, and feeling the things of this world, including your own body, for the very first time. Experience being reborn to the world around you and in you with heightened appreciation for the newness of each moment. Practice this a few times today in various situations.

CHAPTER TWO

BEIT

(bayt)

SOUND: *b* or *v*

NUMERICAL VALUE: 2

Meanings

בית, *Beit*, means "house of" and *bayit*, its cousin with the same Hebrew root, means "house" or "home." *Beit* is the first letter of the word הכרב, *bracha*, "blessing." *Beit*, written large, is the very first letter of the Torah, בראשית, *bereishit* — "In the beginning." The whole Torah thus begins with the energy of blessing and the shelter of a home.

For the nomadic early Jews, houses were tents, temporary dwelling places. For hundreds of years, Jews wandered, at home in their tents, praying in their tabernacles, but at the same time yearning for a homeland, searching for a settled home. They also longed, as Isaiah put it, that "My house shall be a house of prayer for all people,"[1] that this house would be a blessing not just for them, but for all.

Application

At some point, all our ancestors, Jewish or not, wandered, or were driven or fled or were forcibly taken far from their original homes. The entire world is in diaspora. Everyone is in some form of exile. Everyone is searching for home.

The letter *Beit* challenges us to sanctify or make holy the place where we presently find ourselves, even as we roam and search and yearn for our true home.

Do we feel the wistfulness, the grief, the displaced feeling of those who are exiled from their homeland? Do we feel ourselves somehow to be, like Moses, "strangers in a strange land"? Do we feel lost, far from home?

If so, *Beit* offers us the hope that we too can find the freedom of our nomadic ancestors, who set up their tents and yurts where they found themselves, and then were at home there in the desert or steppes, amid the changing landscapes of their lives.

The Japanese haiku poet Bashō wrote in the seventeenth century,

> Journeying through the world
> To and fro, to and fro
> Cultivating a small field.[2]

In the midst of his pilgrimages back and forth across the Japanese countryside, Bashō found his place of home, his field of cultivation, right there before him. We can find ours too.

Shortly after moving to southern Oregon after living in Portland for twenty-one years, I returned to Portland to visit my friend, the author and historian, Terence O'Donnell, one last time before he died. Terence asked how I liked living in Ashland. I said it felt strange to me, and I felt displaced and a little lost. "Bloom where you're planted," was Terry's gentle advice.

This is good *Beit* wisdom.

One way to bloom where we're planted, to feel more at home in the world, is to feel at home in our bodies. Breathing fully and deeply is a key way to do this. Breathing into our bellies, we come home to ourselves. We can take a complete breath right now. We can practice deep, yet gentle, belly breathing every day. For example, we can take a full breath each time the phone rings before we pick up the receiver. We can take some deep breaths when we're waiting for the traffic light to turn green or standing in an elevator. We can find regular, daily opportunities to really settle there in the *Beit* of our bellies.

Beit calls us to recognize the beauty, the wonder, the holiness of our physical selves just as they are, no matter their size or weight or height. At the same time, it can inspire us to take the steps necessary to protect and nurture and heal our bodies, for example by being mindful of the foods we invite in to the holy houses, these alchemical containers, of our bodies.

Beit can also be a reminder to care for the body of the earth, the house of the earth, the temple of the earth. The letter is a cue to be mindful of outer as well as inner ecological balance.

Beit is open to the left, open to the future (since Hebrew reads from right to left). This reminds us to remain open to receive guests, whether they be travelers or new ideas. Our models are Abraham and Sarah, whose tent had no walls and who spontaneously welcomed three strangers, not realizing they were angels in human form. *Beit* encourages us to open ourselves to the give-and-take of human community and spirit community, and welcome angels, the "messengers of the Most High," into our consciousness.

As we do this welcoming, the walls of our inner houses expand, and our homes become *Beitim Midrashim*, sanctuaries of study and learning.

Reading and studying and talking bring us only so far, however. It is possible to move beyond the realm of words and reason, beyond even the idea of oneness, into direct, vivid experience of now. The sixteenth-century Japanese Zen master Hakuin wrote, "With form that is no form, coming and going you never leave home."[3] *Ein Sof* is a term for the ultimate nothingness of God. Touching the realm beyond form, the *Ein Sof* of the Holy One, we are always at home.

Letting go of our preconceived ideas, not being attached to our thoughts, noticing the ground under our feet and the open sky above us, we can be at home with the changing circumstances of our lives. Then, our houses, no matter how flimsy or humble, become houses of prayer for all people, blessings to all.

When we spend some time in *Beit*, we are called to ponder the nature of blessing. What does it mean to bless? What does it mean to be blessed? God promised Avram that he would be a blessing. How can we be blessings? One way is to count our blessings. Feeling blessed opens the way for us to find tangible ways to bless others.

At the same time, as Martín Prechtel reminds us, until the unblessed become the blessers, there will never be peace or wholeness.

Naomi Shihab Nye writes in her poem, "Kindness," "Before you know what kindness really is/you must lose things,/feel the future dissolve in a moment/like salt in a weakened broth."[4]

Those who have lost their loved ones or their homes know best how precious these gifts are. A blessing from one of these holy beings is a powerful blessing indeed.

Beit challenges each of us to maintain an intention of blessing, and an awareness of having been blessed, as we journey to and fro through the landscapes of our lives.

Beit's Shadow

There is danger in taking too literally the desire for one's house to be a house of prayer for all people. The belief that one's spiritual home is better than all others, that one's mode of religious practice deserves to become predominant, has been the justification for wars, persecutions, and atrocities throughout history.

Nowadays there is even violence to Jews against other Jews who have different views of what it means to be a Jew. This is an example of the danger that inevitably accompanies such chauvinistic thinking. This kind of thinking stems from the grief of having lost our homes. We impose our beliefs onto others in an attempt to create a place where we might feel settled. *Beit* reminds us to be alert to the tendency within ourselves of any feelings of self-righteous superiority.

Personal Comments

In the early 1900s, my grandparents fled pogroms and persecution in Poland and the Ukraine and sailed to the United States. Like so many Jewish immigrants, they settled in New York. They made homes there, amid the tall buildings and subways and millions of people, marrying, raising children, finding jobs. And, half a century later, I was born, another native of New York.

But as I got older, I felt native to no place. I was increasingly lost in this strange New World of New York. You couldn't see the stars at night — too many lights. You couldn't see the sunrise or the sunset — too many tall buildings. You couldn't follow streams — they had disappeared under the concrete. And me, where did I belong? Where was my place?

Beit reminds me of home. It carries the faint smell of something very old, which at one time was very familiar. *Beit* encourages me that yes, even in this strange country of modern-day USA, I can still sniff a little bit of that powerful smell, the original smell, and once again be at home on the face of the earth.

ב
Summary for Beit

Numerical value:	2
Meanings:	House. Blessing. Container.
Application:	Bloom where we're planted.
	Breathe into the belly to find our home.
	Make one's home a *Beit Midrash*, a house of study.
	Count one's blessings and be a blessing.
	Seek blessings from the "unblessed."
Shadow:	Feeling spiritually superior to other people.
Reflection:	What are three specific ways in which I can be a blessing today?
Suggested action:	Speaking aloud, bless someone today.

CHAPTER THREE

GIMMEL

(gim'mul)

SOUND: *g*

NUMERICAL VALUE: 3

Meanings

Gimmel is the third letter of the *Aleph Beit*. It shares the same Hebrew root, **גמל**, as the word *gamal*, "camel." The shape of the letter, with its long neck, suggests a camel, and the English word derives from its ancient Semitic ancestor. A related word is *gamol*, "nourished until completely ripe or weaned."

The Talmud teaches that the foot of the letter *Gimmel* is running toward *Dalet* (the next letter in the *Aleph Beit*), which means "poor," as a wealthy person runs after a needy person to do kindness to him or her.

Gimmel represents the number three. It is a letter of stability and equilibrium, like a three-legged stool. At the same time, *Gimmel* is the mysterious third thing that comes into being after the one of *Aleph* and the two of *Beit*.

Robert Bly's poem, "The Third Body," invokes this elusive third entitity that arises from the merging of two. The poem says a man and a woman:

> obey a third body they have in common.
> They have made a promise to love that body.
> Age may come, parting may come, death will come.
> A man and woman sit near each other;
> as they breathe they feed someone we do not know,
> someone we know of, whom we have never seen.[1]

The Hebrew word for "bridge," גשר, gesher, begins with the letter *Gimmel*. With *Gimmel* we are able to create a bridge, bringing the unity of *Aleph* and the duality of *Beit* into a kind of inner balance. This synthesis or marriage prepares the way for action in the world in the form of *g'milut chasadim*, "deeds of loving-kindness." (Rabbi Julia Melanie Vaughns points out that *gemal*, the root of *g'milut chasadim*, means requital, recompense, remuneration. It implies a responsibility to give back for the love and sustenance you have received.)

The Talmud declares that the world stands on three foundations — Torah, prayer, and deeds of loving-kindness.[2] We could say that *Aleph* represents the central teaching of the Torah that God is one, *Beit* represents the house of prayer and blessing, and *Gimmel* the third foundation, that of good deeds.

Application

When we select *Gimmel*, we are being led to investigate our "camel nature," the ability to nourish ourselves and others, and thereby perform deeds of loving-kindness.

A camel is a remarkable animal. It can journey long distances through the desert, going for days without drinking, carrying within itself an internal source of nourishment and replenishment. (Camels do this by metabolizing the fat stored in their humps and converting it into water.)

Gimmel encourages us that even though we may be traveling through a hot, dry, intimidating desert, we already have within us the resources we need to survive.

Not only do we have enough for our own needs, we have enough to share with others and do acts of kindness. *Gimmel* affirms that we are "wealthy." With this abundance, the desire to share naturally wells up within us.

The late Rabbi Shlomo Carlebach tells a moving story about meeting a hunchbacked street cleaner in Israel who as a child had been a student of the famous "Rebbe of the Warsaw Ghetto," Kalonymus Kalman Shapira. The street sweeper describes how Reb Kalonymus would always end his teachings by saying, "*Kinderlech*, children, precious children, remember, the greatest thing in the world is to do somebody else a favor."

This teaching gave the street cleaner the strength to resist suicide and survive the Auschwitz concentration camp. "Do you know how many favors you can do at night at Auschwitz?" he asks Shlomo. Then, this teaching helps him resist despair and the temptation to kill himself in Tel Aviv. "Do you know how many favors you can do on the streets of the world?" he says.[3]

This street cleaner, hunchbacked (like a camel) from being beaten at Auschwitz, found his own nourishment and ability to continue living through performing deeds of loving-kindness. *Gimmel* reminds us all, "*Kinderlech*, children, remember, the greatest thing in the world is to do somebody else a favor." (And, remember, this "somebody else" doesn't necessarily have to be human.)

This sign of the camel may indicate that one has recently gone, or is still going, through a "desert" experience of some sort. These may take the form of lack of money, health, friends, or inspiration. *Gimmel* encourages us to believe in our own internal resources. Like the camel, we have what we need within us. Even though, like a camel, we may proceed slowly, we may move awkwardly, we may have difficulty getting started, nonetheless we are making steady progress through the desert. *Gimmel* gives us the reassurance that we will make it through.

We have enough to make it through, *and* we have enough to share.

Jewish teachings enumerate specific good deeds such as burying the dead, escorting a bride to her wedding canopy, visiting the sick, comforting mourners, planting trees. There are infinite additional ways to feed the world, from small acts of kindness to grand, noble projects. Maybe offering a joke at the right time, or a smile, or silent listening, or a kind touch, or food, or water is just the thing needed to nourish one who is thirsting for hope or renewal.

Much of modern society seems to be lost in a cultural desert. *Gimmel* shows that, just as the camel travels through the desert with its nourishment contained within, we have the gifts we need to thrive in this cultural desert. This letter suggests that we can find ways to bring nourishment to our increasingly barren collective culture. Our art, music, poems, or stories, or any work of beauty can feed the soul hungry for culture, and can feed Spirit itself. Bringing this forth into the world as an offering to the Divine and to the people can be one of the greatest acts of loving-kindness one can perform.

Gimmel also calls us to honor the "wealth" that arises, paradoxically, when we let everything go — our attachment to ideas about God, comparisons of people, conceptions about ourselves.

When we let ourselves relax in this way into the empty fullness of *Ein Sof*, the "Without End-ness" of the Holy, even for a few moments, we find a tremendous liberation of energy and a natural outpouring of compassion. This liberation nourishes us, and this compassion becomes the nourishment or charity we carry out into the world. When we choose *Gimmel*, we are asked to release our grasp on the reins of tightly held concepts, and let our camel nature naturally walk us along the ancient paths.

Gimmel's Shadow

One shadow of *Gimmel* is described by the saying "The road to hell is paved with good intentions." Running after someone to do him or her good may lead to some very bad results. Some missionaries, convinced of the purity of their motivations, nonetheless brought disease and cultural destruction to the native peoples they sought to convert.

To think of oneself as a rich person who is going to help a poor person can set up a dynamic of resentment and anger on the part of both the giver and the receiver, and one's actions can backfire. *Gimmel* calls for skillful means of performing good deeds. One way to achieve this is to let go of the notion of "good deeds" entirely, and just do what is before us to the best of our ability.

Personal Comments

Have you ever ridden on a camel, listening to the melancholy sound of the wooden camel bells as you bounce and sway along the hot and dusty track? This sign of the camel, *Gimmel*, carries me when I get discouraged. It carries me when I'm lost. It carries me when I'm feeling so low that I forget I have anything to offer anyone. *Gimmel* reminds me that the way to refreshment is action.

Summary for Gimmel

Numerical value:	3
Meanings:	Camel. Good deeds.
Application:	Know that we have the strength and endurance we need.
	Perform deeds of loving-kindness.
	Feed the culture and the Divine through our art and creativity.
Shadow:	Misguided missionary zeal.
Reflection:	What are some opportunities for loving-kindness that arise in the course of an ordinary day? How can I act on these opportunities more consistently?
Suggested action:	Perform a tangible act of loving-kindness today.

CHAPTER FOUR

DALET

(dah'let)

SOUND: *d*

NUMERICAL VALUE: 4

Meanings

The fourth letter of the *Aleph Beit*, *Dalet* shares the same Hebrew root as דלת, *delet*, meaning "door," "doorway," "entrance," "threshold." The form of *Dalet* suggests an open doorway with its horizontal top or lintel and vertical doorpost.

Dalet is also said to suggest a person doubled over while carrying a heavy load. This is related to the other main association with *Dalet*, that of a poor person who knocks on doors, begging for alms. As discussed in the chapter on *Gimmel*, the Talmud describes *Dalet* as a poor person toward whom *Gimmel* is rushing in order to give charity.

Application

When *Dalet* wanders into our life, we are asked to examine the nature of true wealth. *Dalet* calls on us to open up our doors to receive the gifts that the universe is rushing to bestow upon us. Our ability to recognize and receive these gifts depends on our humility. It's not easy to acknowledge that we are needy and to allow ourselves to accept offerings from others. When we are not full of self-importance, when we are poor in ego and opinions, then the doorway is open for inspiration and divine gifts to flow into our lives.

Selecting *Dalet* is a reminder to cultivate humility. Have we become arrogant, puffed up with our own importance, forgetting to acknowledge the central place of the Divine? The word "humility" comes from *humus*, meaning "earth." The English word "human" has a similar etymology, as does the Hebrew word אדם, *adam*, which indicates both "man" and "earth" (and is the name of the first man on earth). As we become more humble, we become more human.

Humility arises from being connected with our roots, down close to the soil. *Dalet*, bent over toward the ground, calls us to remember this connection, that our bodies and nurturance, our very lives, depend on the earth. In fact, our bodies *are* the earth. We are the earth manifesting as living, moving, self-aware and reflective creatures. We are not separate, and we are not self-sufficient. Rather, we are connected to and dependent upon everything.

If we are going through a difficult time and feeling low and poor, *Dalet* can be an encouragement that this very difficulty can be the door through which greater blessings will enter. As Jesus said, "Blessed are the poor in spirit: for theirs is the kingdom of heaven."

Receiving gifts and blessings gracefully can itself be a gift offered to others. The Talmud says that more than a baby seeks to be nursed does a mother seek to nurse her baby. Sometimes we give, sometimes we receive. Sometimes the door swings one way, sometimes the other. As we remain open to each situation, not burdened by either inflated ideas of ourselves on one hand or excessively self-condemnatory ones on the other, we find the appropriate response.

Our senses are the doors of our bodies. As we open them more fully, blessings naturally flow. These blessings grace us with the riches of the material world, in such forms as a bird's call, sunlight glinting on green leaves, the smell of onions, the taste of an apple. When our time is full of busyness and the arrogant pursuit of "more important" matters, and our minds are full of ideas, we shut the door on these simple blessings, this humble daily life which after all is our only life.

Doorways mark borders. They define "in" and "out." Modern-day seer Paul Richards teaches that energy gathers at borders. These can be physical borders such as where the ocean meets the land, or temporal borders, such as New Year's or a wedding or the end of a job. Humble yet powerful *Dalet* is right at the center of these energy-rich boundaries. It's the guardian of transitions, the open doorway between one environment and another, between what has been and what might be.

In traditional villages in the Mayan highlands of Guatemala, the houses have doorways but no doors. In fact, there is no word in the Mayan language for "door." Doorways allow for the free flow of sounds and sights and people in and out of the house, each household connected to the rest of the village in a natural and familiar age-old pattern. In recent decades, after doors were introduced to many of these traditional villages, people started guarding their belongings more and sharing less; informal socializing decreased, thievery increased. Soon everyone started putting locks on the doors and keeping them shut. The social fabric of the villages became frayed.[1]

One of *Dalet*'s messages for us is to find ways to stay open to our villages. While our doorways define inside and outside and provide important protection, closed and locked doors can block the healthy circulation of people and ideas.

Dalet asks us to open the doors to our hearts. The suffering of the world and the pain in our own lives can lead us to shut down, to close the door on these difficult emotions. *Dalet* encourages us to have the courage to confront these feelings, to open up to them. "Courage" comes from *coeur*, the French word for heart. It is courageous to feel with our hearts the distress of the world. Much of our lives and modern culture is actually built on distracting us from confronting this pain.

Simple, heartfelt prayers carry tremendous power. One teacher of old wrote, "Do not think that the words of prayer as you say them go up to God. It is not the words themselves that ascend; it is rather the burning desire of your heart that rises like smoke toward heaven. If your prayer consists only of words and letters, and does not contain your heart's desire — how can it rise up to God?"[2] *Dalet* gives us the reassurance that as we offer our prayers humbly and sincerely, wisdom and creativity will flow toward us.

One *Rosh Hashanah*, the Baal Shem Tov instructed his disciple Reb Wolf Kitzes in the proper way to blow the *shofar*, the ram's horn. The Baal Shem taught him the specific *kavanot* or prayerful intentions the student would need to concentrate on with each blow. But when the time in the service for the blowing arrived, poor, nervous Reb Wolf forgot all the *kavanot* and all the prayers. It was all he could do to manage to blow the *shofar* in the proper sequence. Afterwards, he was miserable, heartbroken, and with tears in his eyes he confessed to the Baal Shem Tov his failure to maintain the proper *kavanah* when blowing the *shofar*.

The Baal Shem Tov comforted him with this allegory: there are many keys to the various doors of God's house. But there is a master key that opens all the doors. This master key is an axe. Each of the *kavanot* for the *shofar* is like one of the keys to the individual doors. The master key, the axe, the Baal Shem Tov taught, is a broken heart. With this master key, one breaks down all the doors and stands directly in the presence of the Divine.[3]

Paradoxically, as we open our hearts to the fullness of grief and sadness, we open ourselves to receive joy as well. The Hasidic masters teach that one of the best ways to do this is through singing and dancing. Rebbe Nachman of Breslav, the great-grandson of the Baal Shem, said, "The most direct means for attaching ourselves to God from this material world is through music and song." He also wrote, "Get into the habit of singing a tune. It will give you new life and fill you with joy." And elsewhere he said, "Get into the habit of dancing. It will displace depression and dispel hardship."[4]

Niggunim, the wordless melodies of the Hasidim, have the quality of opening the doors of our hearts to simultaneous feelings of joy and grief. We can incorporate the message of *Dalet* by learning and singing regularly some of these simple and beautiful songs.

One way *Dalet's* poverty or humbleness manifests is in freedom from feeling attached to a separated sense of self. As we let go of the barriers between us and "others," us and God, a profound openness results. The doors are thrown wide open. Walt Whitman exhorted us to "Unscrew the locks from the doors!/Unscrew the doors themselves from their jambs!"

Dalet represents the number four. Four is a number of wholeness, fullness, and completion. There are four elements, four cardinal directions, four seasons, four Worlds in Kabbalistic cosmology, and four letters in God's Holy Name, *Yud/Hei/Vav/Hei*. Paradoxically, the impoverished and needy *Dalet* embodies this number of wholeness. Letting go of everything, owning nothing, poor *Dalet* receives the blessings of the whole universe. In its very emptiness, *Dalet* becomes full.

Dalet encourages us to not be afraid to be "poor in Spirit." It promises profound fullness and completion, with the four elements, four directions, four seasons, and the Holy Name all conspiring to pour forth new blessings through the doorways of our lives.

Dalet's Shadow

One of *Dalet's* shadows is that of false humility. Do we nurse a desire to be praised for how noble we are for our sacrifices or modest outward behavior? Are we proud of how humble we are? Selecting this letter can be a reminder to be alert to this subtle tendency.

Another shadow of *Dalet* is excessive humility. Lack of self-esteem is epidemic in our culture, leading to depression and self-destructive behaviors. In many cases, a little less humility and a little more pride may be exactly what is called for.

Personal Comments

Hello *Dalet*. One reason Jews have *mezzuzot* on their doors is to remind them that thresholds are sacred. Coming in and going out, that's what our lives are made of. Breath comes in and goes out our lungs, blood comes in and goes out our hearts, ideas come in and go out our minds — in and out, in and out.

My grandfather had a plan for getting into heaven. He would stand at the gates of heaven and open the gate and close the gate, open the gate and close the gate, open the gate and close the gate. Finally, the guardian of the gates would yell in exasperation, "Look, either in or out!" and my grandfather would go in.

Dalet, on the other hand, is both in and out, neither in nor out. It represents the freedom of the threshold. At the threshold all things are new. At the threshold anything is possible. Our treasure is right here, at the threshold!

ד

Summary for Dalet

Numerical value:	4
Meanings:	Door. Doorway. Threshold. Humility.
Application:	Open the doors of our senses.
	Stay open to our village.
	Open our hearts to grief and joy.
	Walk humbly.
Shadow:	False humility.
	Excessive humility.
Reflection:	What is the "burning desire of my heart that rises like smoke toward heaven"? How can I act more fully in accord with this desire?
Suggested action:	Find a way today to open yourself more to a situation or person to which the door of your heart is closed.

CHAPTER FIVE

HEI

(hay)

SOUND: *h*

NUMERICAL VALUE: 5

Meanings

The name of the fifth letter of the *Aleph Beit*, הא, *Hei*, means "lo" or "behold."

Hei is the letter most often linked with God's name, as in יה, *Yah*. The most sacred configuration of the Holy Name, יהוה, *Yud-Hei-Vav-Hei* or YHVH, contains two *Hei's*.

Hei is one of the mildest-sounding of the letters. Its sound is the merest breath or exhalation. As a suffix, *Hei* denotes the feminine form of a noun.

Application

When *Hei* whispers its way into our awareness, we can be sure that we are in a holy state, close to the Holy Name, near to the mothering aspect of the Divine. This closeness may take the outward form of broken hopes or relationships, however. *Hei* is one of only two letters in the *Aleph Beit* formed of two unattached or broken parts. But *Hei* offers the assurance that, just as a seed must break open within the mother earth in order to sprout, we are being cracked open in order to bring new life into being.

Hei says, "Lo and behold, here it is! Right here within you and before you is the expression, the very manifestation of the Divine."

The Torah reports that God indicates faith in Avram and Sarai by adding *Hei*, the initial of God, to their names. Sarai, שרי, thus becomes Sarah, שרה, and Avram, אברם, becomes Avraham, אברהם. After this, despite their extreme age, Avraham is able to impregnate Sarah, and Sarah is able to conceive and bear Yitzhak, Isaac, ushering in the long line of the Hebrew people. The letter *Hei* helps sanctify Avraham and Sarah, symbolizing their fitness to manifest new life unexpectedly and miraculously, affecting the destiny of the whole world.

Hei can also transform us. Isaac's name means "laughter" and "delight." In many languages all around the world, words that indicate laughter commonly begin with the *Hei* sound, such as "ha" and "ho" and "hee." As the soft but powerful effects of *Hei* inform our lives, as it did for Avraham and Sarah, a period of barrenness can end, and happiness and the sounds of laughter and delight resound through our houses once again.

In addition to meaning "lo" or "behold," *Hei*, as a prefix, stands for the definite article "the." The Talmud says that God used the letters *Yud* and *Hei*, which comprise the holy name יה, *Yah*, to create the universe. The *Yud* was used to create the "World to Come" and the *Hei* was used to create "This World." If *Hei* has manifested in our awareness, we are being asked to pay attention to what is before us, to behold the actual stuff of our life, to be grounded in This World.

Hei as "the" is a *definite* article; it refers to a specific object or thing, not just a generality or abstraction. Have we become lost in abstractions, alienated from our bodies, our physical experience? *Hei* reminds us to pay attention to the specific, definite aspects of our lives.

Rebbe Nachman once spotted one of his followers rushing by. "Have you looked up at the sky this morning?" the *rebbe* asked. "No, Rebbe, I haven't had the time." "Believe me, in fifty years everything you see here today will be gone. There will be another fair — with other horses, other wagons, different people. I won't be here then and neither will you. So what's so important that you don't have time to look at the sky?"[1]

In a similar vein, the author Simone Weil once wrote, "Prayer consists of attention."[2]

Our attention is among our most precious possessions. How and where we put our attention is one of the most crucial choices we make moment to moment in our lives. There are so many forces vying for our attention, often without our best interests in mind. Paul Richards has said that one of the travesties of the 9/11 attacks was that the terrorists stole the collective attention of the world and riveted it on their acts of destruction.

To what will we pay attention? It is possible to put *what we love* in the center of our attention. To focus on our own and others' greatness instead of mediocrity. On creation instead of destruction. This kind of wielding of attention does not mean being blind or ignorant or living in a state of denial. It does mean respecting the profound treasure that our attention represents. When we have what we love in the center of our attention, then we can look at the troubling aspects of life without getting consumed by those aspects and lost in them.

My friend and guide, Ernie Thayer, goes a step further. He teaches that the entire universe itself is comprised of "warm, curious attention." Attention is not just a personal quality that we wield with varying degrees of effectiveness. It's not *our* attention, per se. Attention is really the universe's attention moving through us. This is hinted at by the double *Hei*'s in the holy name, *Yud Hei Vav Hei.*

Moses was one person who paid attention. One day while tending his father-in-law's flocks, Moses sees a fire coming out of a bush. As he looks, he realizes the bush is not being consumed by the fire. Moses says, "I must go over there and investigate this wonderful phenomenon. Why doesn't the bush burn?"

Moses was in the right place at the right time to become aware of this strange sight. What's more, he was attentive to it, able to notice it in the first place, and then willing to interrupt his plans and turn aside to investigate it. He wasn't so caught up in his own thoughts and preoccupations that he missed this opportunity to become more intimate with the Holy.

The Torah continues, "When God saw that Moses was going to investigate, God called to him from the middle of the bush: 'Moses! Moses!' "Moses answered, 'Here I am.'"

This "Here I am," or הנני, *hineni*, exemplifies the power of *Hei*.

God then says to Moses, "Take your shoes off your feet. The place upon which you are standing is holy ground."[3]

This is the message of *Hei*: Holiness is right here! The place on which we stand, wherever we stand, is holy ground. The bush is still burning. The fire of immediacy flames bright and hot. The question is whether or not we will pay attention and notice. Life is continuously giving us the opportunity to respond *hineni*! Lo and behold, right here, in this very body, this very place, is the Divine.

The English word "hey" is directly related to its Hebrew cousin. *Hei* calls out for attention, "Hey! Here it is! It's no longer hidden!" The English word "aha!" carries the energy of *Hei*. We can be alert for "aha!"-type experiences, where suddenly something clicks, where suddenly we "get it." One sign that this has happened is an inflowing of laughter and delight.

On the other hand, revelations may come quietly and subtly, whispering their way into our awareness. The prophet Elijah, in desperate straits, fled to the wilderness and was led to stand upon Mount Horeb. At the mountain top, "*Adonai* passed by. There was a great and mighty wind, splitting mountains and shattering rocks by the power of *Adonai*; but *Adonai* was not in the wind. After the wind — an earthquake; but *Adonai* was not in the earthquake. After the earthquake — fire; but *Adonai* was not in the fire. And after the fire — a soft murmuring sound." Sometimes this is translated as "a still, small voice."[4]

Amid the clamor of the world, the turmoil of our lives, that voice of *Hei* is quietly breathing, murmuring its soft but powerful sound. Much of our lives is consumed by the whirlwind of thoughts and ideas, the earthquake of actions, the fire of emotions. *Hei* indicates a time to turn away from all that and attend to the small sound of the Divine.

As we sigh deeply, voicing the "haaaah" of *Hei* and stilling our minds and bodies, we prepare ourselves to hear or feel the soft murmuring sound of divine inspiration echo in our bellies. Doing this, we make ourselves ready to hear messages from on high.

Then we can come down from the mountain, renewed and refreshed, ready to engage the world once again, birthing new beauty and delight into being.

Hei's Shadow

One danger of *Hei*, this broken letter, is getting stuck in brokenness. Broken hearts, like broken bones, can cripple us. Our challenge is to let the broken aspects of our lives inform our wholeness, adding not despair and hopelessness but depth and maturity to our nature.

Another shadow comes with "the soft murmuring sound." Distinguishing divine inspiration from self-deception is not always easy. Tempering confidence in our revelations with a little humility can help us avoid the common trap of imposing our vision onto others in a destructive or arrogant fashion.

Personal Comments

Much of the time, I walk around in kind of a daze, my mind filled with daydreams and plans and speculations and worries, not really noticing the vibrant life moving and speaking all around me. But every now and then, somehow, the energy of *Hei* penetrates my mental chatter and calls out, "Hey! Wake up! Pay attention!" And then, almost despite myself, I notice the slant of the sunlight, the feel of the breeze, the deep blast of the train whistle, the smell of the popcorn. *Hei* awakens me, and for those vivid moments, I am able to say, with conviction, "*Hineni*! Here I am!"

Summary for Hei

Numerical value: 5

Meanings: Lo! Behold! The. *Hineni*, "Here I am."

Application: Pay attention.

Listen for the still, small voice.

Shadow: Becoming stuck in brokenness.

Self-deception.

Reflection: What is the "soft murmuring sound" of the Divine saying to me today?

Suggested action: At least three times today, take three deep breaths, look up, look down, look all around, and say out loud, "*Hineni*! Here I am!"

CHAPTER SIX

VAV

(vahv)

SOUND: *v* or *w*

NUMERICAL VALUE: 6

Meanings

וו, the name of *Vav*, the sixth letter of the *Aleph Beit*, means "hook." As a prefix to a noun, *Vav* means "and."

In Biblical Hebrew, when used as a prefix to a verb, *Vav* serves a special function; it changes the tense of the verb from past to future or vice versa. In this role, *Vav* inverts time, connecting and transmuting past and future.

Vav equals the number six, the number of days in which the universe was created.

Application

Vav is an incredibly powerful letter of connection, of continuity, of unification through both time and space. When *Vav* connects with us, it is an opportunity to deepen our sense of unity and connection with all things.

One of the diseases of our time is feeling disconnected. Many of us lack a deep intimacy with the physical place where we live, the animals, plants, rivers, hills, rocks, and insects of our specific bioregions. We're often disconnected from neighbors, family members, friends. We're sometimes disconnected from our own bodies and our own emotions. We may feel disconnected from the realm of our ancestors. Often, we feel disconnected from God.

In fact, we spend much of our lives trying somehow to connect, to break down the walls of apparent separation. *Vav*, as one of the twenty-two letter energies with which the Holy created the universe, offers the encouragement that the power of connection is built deeply into the very structure of creation.

Vav's energy of connection is embedded in the most sacred configuration of God's name, יהוה, *Yud-Hei-Vav-Hei*. *Vav* shows us that, in fact, we may not be as separate as we feel. In fact, we may not be separate at all. This does not mean losing our individuality or uniqueness as sentient beings. It just means that we are not isolated and alone.

How do we foster a *Vav*-like sense of connection at the physical level? One way is to become conscious of the pull of gravity of our body center to the center of the earth. We are connected, center-to-center, belly-to-belly, with this spinning planet on which we live. We can take a few moments to bend our knees slightly, plant our feet firmly on the ground, and move our body center closer to the earth's center. Then, we can feel the power of the earth entering up through our feet and legs all the way to our belly even as gravity hugs us down.

Our feet dwell down there at the mysterious edge, the border between us and the planet. They walk us through our lives, along the surface of the world, while our body's core forms the *Vav* of connection with the core of the world, thus connecting us to everyone and everything else on this globe.

Even when we're not aware of such a connection, we are indeed connected. In fact, it is possible to break down a sense of duality between us and the planet, and experience our walking as the earth itself walking, our breathing, or being breathed, as the planet breathing.

The act of eating is a profound act of uniting. The plants and animals and liquids we take into our bodies mysteriously become "us." At the Passover table we unite with our ancestors when we taste the bitter herbs of affliction and the dryness of the unleavened *matzah* of the desert.

It was at a Passover *seder* that Jesus and his disciples ate the "Last Supper." Jesus' sharing of the *matzah* and the wine became the prototype for the sacrament of communion. Actually, every time we eat or drink or even breathe, we are partaking in communion, coming into union with the sun, the rain, the soil, the life force of plant or animal, the ancestors of that plant or animal, and also with the energies of the humans who raised the food, transported it, sold it, cooked it.

In acknowledgment of all this, observant Jews wash their hands and say a blessing each time before eating, and say prayers of thanks afterwards. Every act of eating or drinking is a miracle: a miracle of connection. Appreciating our food in this way, we feed our *Vav* awareness at the same time we nourish our bodies.

Through its energy of connection and unification, *Vav* helps heal a ruptured universe. Led by the sixteenth-century rabbi, Isaac Luria, the Kabbalists developed an idea known as "the shattering of the vessels." In the beginning, God emanated divine light. In order for this light to be accessible to the finite world, it was poured into vessels corresponding to the ten *Sefirot*, or branches, of the Tree of Life. The vessels of the three highest branches were able to contain the light, but when it entered the lower branches, the great power of the divine light was too much for the vessels and they broke and the light was scattered.

Since that time, a fundamental responsibility of humans is to work at *tikkun*, repair of the vessels and the unification of the scattered and exiled shards of light. The appearance of the Messiah will mark the consummation of this ongoing process of restoration.

When the last vessel shattered, the *Shechinah*, the feminine, immanent aspect of the Divine, was driven into exile. *Tikkun* seeks to reunite the *Shechinah*, the Divine Bride, with the masculine, transcendent aspect of the Divine. The scholar Gershom Scholem writes that "in one way or other the true purpose of the Torah" is to lead the *Shechinah* back to union with God.[1] Rabbi Luria taught that the fulfillment of each of the 613 commandments should be accompanied with the declaration that the act was done for the sake of uniting the Holy One and the *Shechinah*.

The shattering of the vessels and the exile of the *Shechinah* parallel the fall from the Garden of Eden. With the shattering of the vessels, God's very nature is split. The male and female parts of the Divine, the transcendent and immanent, are exiled from each other. No wonder we humans feel a void or separation within ourselves. No wonder there is such a gulf and such tension between men and women.

Vav forwards the process of *tikkun*. It embraces opposites. As the saying goes, "These and these are true."

Ironically, one of these seeming opposites is that while the world is broken, at the same time there is nothing to repair! It just is what it is. Maybe *tikkun* is realizing, not just intellectually but vividly and viscerally, that all is okay, that it's all going to be all right.

Vav gathers together the scattered sparks of divine light from the six corners of the universe and from past and future. By selecting *Vav*, one is called to be part of the great unifying process of *tikkun*. Each person has a key role to play in bringing together the sparks of divinity, of uniting the Bride and the Groom, healing the rift between woman and man. *Vav* inspires us to become agents of connection, of re-union to help usher in the messianic age in which exile is ended, the vessels of divine light are repaired, and wholeness and harmony reign.

Vav encourages us to find our special place in the process of restoring the light of creation. How will we help forward *tikkun*? This is our challenge and our destiny. Some people attempt *tikkun olam*, "repair of the world," in a very practical way through political participation, environmental action, community involvement. Others approach the challenge of *tikkun* more mystically. *Vav* conveys the general quality of the process, namely connection and unification. Through our prayers and actions performed with *kavanah*, intention, we contribute, each in our unique way, to this cosmic repair job.

Vav's Shadow

Getting "hooked" is one of the negative sides of *Vav*. Addictions of all sorts are a kind of over-connectedness. Are we addicted to novelty, to praise, to work, to stimulation, to our own personal melodramas?

Are we over-identified with another person? It's wonderful to have a profound connection with someone, but how easily that connection can slip into an unhealthy codependence. There is a time for consensus and there is a time to take strong, unilateral action. *Vav* serves as a reminder to nurture and welcome our connections to others, while not neglecting to nurture our own unique individuality as well.

Personal Comments

Sometimes I wander about the city streets, and people seem so different from me. I feel cut off from them, cut off from the land, cut off from my ancestors, cut off from myself.

In moments of grace, though, *Vav* comes to my aid. *Vav* reminds me that at the roots we are connected, at the roots we are actually part of the same tree. *Vav* is upright like a tree. Trees connect heaven and earth. *Vav* connects you and me. The fruits of this tree are beauty and life. *Vav* prods me to look beneath the surface appearance and see the web of connection all around me. By connecting me to all things, *Vav* connects me to myself.

ו
Summary for Vav

Numerical value:	6
Meanings:	Hook. And. Connection.
Application:	Connect to the earth through the feet.
	Feed our connection as we feed our bodies.
	Discover one's path of *tikkun*, repair.
Shadow:	Getting hooked.
	Codependence.
Reflection:	What are some ways I can forward the process of connection, of re-union, of *tikkun*?
Suggested action:	For a few minutes today, sit quietly and watch your breath. As you do so, imagine yourself not so much breathing as being breathed. This is the ever-present activity of *Ruach Ha-olam*, Spirit of the World (one of the names of God).

CHAPTER SEVEN

ZAYIN

(zi'yin)

SOUND: *z*

NUMERICAL VALUE: 7

Meanings

Zayin is a letter of assertiveness and power. Its form resembles a sword and its name is related to זין, the Hebrew root for "arms" or "weapons."

Zayin equals seven. Seven represents one form of completeness. We commonly describe six physical directions — east, west, north, south, up, and down — plus a seventh, an inward direction, an inner focal point. God rested on the seventh day, having completed the outward work of creating the universe. As the seventh letter of the *Aleph Beit*, *Zayin* symbolizes *Shabbat*, Sabbath, the period we set aside to rest and remember and celebrate that original day of rest and celebration when all things were new.

Zayin is thus a paradox. This sign of a weapon of war is also a symbol of the peace of the *Shabbat*. The challenge with *Zayin* is to integrate the two. Can we be "peaceful warriors"? Can we wield our swords appropriately, defending and inspiring life and beauty instead of causing more death, destruction, and alienation? As with each of the letters of the *Aleph Beit*, the deeper meaning of the letter itself gives guidance on how to meet the challenge.

Application

זכר, *zachor*, "remember," begins with a *Zayin*. "Remember the Sabbath day, to keep it holy," was one of the Ten Commandments, more accurately translated as "Ten Utterances," that Moses brought down from the mountain.[1] As we honor the Sabbath, in the form that feels appropriate, we re-member it, in the sense of piecing it back together again. On *Shabbat*, we re-create our selves as we re-member original creation.

One way to do this is to step out of the world of hustle and bustle, out of commerce and workaday time, out of modernity itself, and enter the sanctuary of sacred time. During *Shabbat*, we rest and welcome into our lives the feminine aspect of the Divine, the *Shechinah*, the Sabbath Queen.

Shabbat is healing for the body and the nervous system, especially in our 24/7 modern world. It's a day to take a break from manual labor and also from technology. The break allows the para-sympathetic nervous system to come forward with what is called "the relaxation response." The vast majority of healing happens during sleep, meditation, and rest, when the holy body can become whole once again.

Choosing *Zayin* can indicate a time to lay low, to stay near home with family and friends, to be with nature, to withdraw from worldly commerce, to study, pray, and sing. The Talmud says, "What was created on the seventh day? Tranquility, serenity, peace, and repose."[2] *Zayin* represents a time to turn to the inner Sabbath, to the seventh, inner direction, and nourish peace.

It's also a time for enjoyment! Abraham Joshua Heschel, in his classic book, *The Sabbath*, teaches, "Unlike the Day of Atonement, the Sabbath is not dedicated exclusively to spiritual goals." It's a day of the body and the soul. "Comfort and pleasure are an integral part of the Sabbath observance."[3]

The Talmud says, "Sanctify the Sabbath by choice meals, by beautiful garments; delight your soul with pleasure and I will reward you for this very pleasure."[4]

We have seen that *Zayin* calls us to remember. Traditionally, the people of the Iroquois League remember not only the ancestors, but those to come. When making any important decision, they consider the children to be born seven generations later. How will this decision affect them?

Zayin reminds us to step back from the day-to-day, and take a look at our lives from this long view. Do we need to adjust anything in our lives today to better serve the seventh generation, which for us now are the children of the late twenty-second century? Do we act as if they matter and that we are responsible to them?

Our ancestors seven generations back lived in the mid 1800s. Did they remember us, their descendants, who are now living in the first part of the twenty-first century?

Shmitah, the sabbatical year, comes every seventh year. *Shmitah* is a period of letting the fields lie fallow and giving the earth a rest. When *Zayin* appears in our hands, it may signify a time to take some form of a sabbatical, to give ourselves a break, at least for a little while, and renew our perspectives, and savor a little freedom.

Freedom, however, often has to be fought for and won, and then defended. Here is where *Zayin* as weapon dovetails with the letter's peaceful, *Shabbat* qualities. To protect our sacred *Shabbat* time, we must wield the sword that guards boundaries. We must defend the precious soul space, protect the feminine aspects of ourselves.

These aspects may be endangered by the demands of other people and our fast-paced materialistic culture, with its patriarchal remnants. We are conditioned to conform to industrial time, not natural time. "Modern time" is 24/7, go! go! go! time. How easily we forget to remember the Sabbath, both literally and figuratively.

Zayin is a call for incisiveness, for that sharp clarity of mind and intention that safeguards that which is precious. Robert Bly says in *Iron John*, "Showing a sword doesn't necessarily mean fighting. It can also suggest a joyous decisiveness."[5]

When Adam and Eve were cast out of the Garden of Eden, a flaming sword was placed at the entrance that turned in every direction and protected the Tree of Life. We are each carriers of the flaming sword that guards the inner tree of life. Through decisiveness in honoring what is truly important to us by cutting off what is not, we skillfully wield the sword of *Zayin*.

William Blake invokes the inspiration of *Zayin* in his preface to *Milton*,

> I will not cease from Mental Fight,
> Nor shall my Sword sleep in my hand,
> Till we have built Jerusalem
> In England's green and pleasant Land.

Choosing the letter *Zayin* is a call to arms. It's a challenge to keep alert and vigilant, and not be lured to sleep by the siren song of commerce and materialism, perfectionism and obsessiveness. We continually have the opportunity to build Jerusalem, *Yerushalayim*, "the Vision of *Shalom*," the city of peace, right here, in this moment, in this body, right where we are.

Zayin's Shadow

The Sabbath comes around only once every seven days. Part of its beauty is in the contrast with the rest of the week. Too much rest and pleasure, too many choice meals, and our lives quickly get out of balance. Laziness and over-indulgence are pitfalls to be aware of when selecting *Zayin*.

Another is over-aggressiveness. It's important to wield the sword that defends boundaries and protects what needs to be protected, but not to become violent or paranoid. *Zayin* evokes that part of human nature that is spoiling for a fight, that longs for blood, that justifies aggression in the name of all sorts of ideologies and rationalizations. When we choose *Zayin*, we are reminded that the dark tendency toward war and violence resides within each of us. By acknowledging the presence of these destructive tendencies in our own natures, we can avoid acting them out or projecting them on to some "other."

Personal Comments

Did you ever pick up a real sword? It's heavy! Yet, there is a way to wield a sword without exhausting oneself, an "effortless effort," or *wu-wei* as they say in Chinese.

Zayin teaches that exhaustion is actually more likely to come if we refuse to pick up that sword which protects our treasure, our sacred time. When I was executive director of Friends of Trees, a nonprofit tree-planting organization, we found ourselves taking on project after project until the staff and volunteers were overstretched and stressed out.

Finally, I posted two signs in the office. One said, "It's the tree-planting, Stupid," to remind us to stay focused on the organization's core mission and help us resist the temptation to stray into extraneous pursuits. The other said, "Just say no to more projects," to discourage us from piling up more and more work for ourselves. Clarifying essential priorities, un-choosing actions that don't align with those priorities, and then being willing to defend our choices and protect our priorities, that's *Zayin* work.

There's a certain kind of sword I became proficient at using. It's light, but effective. You can use it too, if you want. It's the word "no."

ז

Summary for Zayin

Numerical value:	7
Meanings:	Weapon. Sword.
Application:	Remember the Sabbath, remember to rest.
	Wield the sword that protects what is precious.
Shadow:	Indolence.
	War and inappropriate aggression.
Reflection:	In order to honor what is truly important to me, is there anything that I need to cut out?
Suggested action:	This weekend, celebrate the Sabbath in ways that are satisfying and meaningful to you, keeping workaday tasks and pressures to a minimum.

CHAPTER EIGHT

CHET

(cheht)

SOUND: *ch* as in *chutzpah*

NUMERICAL VALUE: 8; INFINITY

Meanings

Chet is the eighth letter of the *Aleph Beit*. As seven is a number of completion, eight signifies a time of new beginnings, the entering of a new cycle. With the eighth day, a new week begins. With the eighth note, a new, higher octave sounds. The Hebrew word for "new," חדש, *chadash*, begins with *Chet*.

Besides standing for the number eight, *Chet* also represents infinity (whose symbol is a sideways eight), the numberless realm beyond space and time.

The form of *Chet* resembles an arch or gateway. New life emerges as we leave the old behind, cross the threshold and step into the unknown, into the infinite.

Such crossings, however, can be full of fear. *Chet* is key to the Hebrew words for both "life," חיים, *chayim*, and "fear," חתה, *chitah*. To be alive is to be afraid. *Chet* teaches us how to negotiate endings and beginnings in our lives in this frightening world with חסד, *chesed*, grace and loving-kindness.

Application

Chet, this powerful symbol of transformation, is the first letter of חפה, *chupah*, the wedding canopy. The form of *Chet* actually looks like a *chupah*. The *chupah* is both a shelter and a gateway into the journey of married life. As the betrothed pair stand beneath the *chupah*, they are in liminal space, a holy, highly-charged, in-between realm. When they emerge from the *chupah*, their lives have been profoundly changed. They are born into the world as a married couple.

Chet evokes these questions: From what metaphorical *chupah* are you emerging? What or whom are you choosing to marry, to unite with? What radical transformations are you undergoing?

At a wedding ceremony, the wine of blessing is drunk and everyone cheers, "*L'chayim!*" "To life!" *Chet* encourages us to stride through the gateway of transformation with a vibrant spirit, to enjoy the spontaneous aliveness of being a human being, to embrace life come what may, good fortune or no.

Come what may. *Gevalt!* Life is a fearsome proposition. One eats and tries to avoid being eaten. Most of us these days are not in danger of being devoured by wild animals, but there are other forces out there that would consume us: microbes, draining jobs, debilitating emotions, illness, drugs and alcohol, consumerism in general, and for everyone ultimately and inevitably, death.

With *Chet*, we cross through a gateway and leave behind naive optimism. *Chet* marks an initiation out of innocence into an awareness of the dangers that underlie our lives. The Book of Job says God "suspends the earth on nothingness."[1] A deep part of us fears falling into or being swallowed up by that abyss of nothing, the infinite void that waits just below our feet, just beyond our next thought, just beyond our next breath.

Nevertheless, *Chet's* animating force is that of *chayim*, life. The challenge is summarized by the title of the book, *Feel the Fear and Do It Anyway*. *Chet* calls us to allow a mature awareness of death and danger to inform and deepen our embrace of life. Death can become an ally, helping us realize the preciousness of life. "A good warrior is always afraid," advises the grandmother in a Modoc Indian tale. *Chutzpah* means "gumption and audacity." *Chet* teaches "holy *chutzpah*," the willingness to make mistakes, to take chances and move into the unknown in order to create something new.

The form of *Chet* suggests a bridge, with the top horizontal line connecting the two vertical ones. Rebbe Nachman of Breslov taught, "All of this world is a very narrow bridge. And above all, have no fear at all." Rebbe Nachman knew about confronting fear. His beloved son died in infancy. The rabbi once undertook a perilous pilgrimage to the Holy Land at the height of the Napoleonic wars. And, for much of his short life he lived with bipolar disorder. Nonetheless, Rebbe Nachman was able to cross the very narrow bridge of his life with good humor, wisdom, and courage, which continue to encourage and enhearten many to this day. He predicted, in fact, that, "my light will glow until the day of the Messiah."

Another Hasidic master, Rabbi Moshe Leib, said, "The way in this world is like the edge of a blade. On this side is the netherworld, and on that side is the netherworld, and the way of life lies in between."[2] The way of life is the way of *Chet*.

Wu-men, a twelfth-century Chinese Zen master, echoes Rebbe Nachman and Rabbi Moshe: "At the very cliff edge of birth and death, you find the Great Freedom."[3] We walk that cliff edge at all times. *Chet* calls us to walk it with *chesed*, grace and loving-kindness, and experience this freedom.

Gary Snyder writes in his poem "Walking Home from 'The Duchess of Malfi'":

> Pains of death and love,
> Birth and war,
>   wreckt earth,
>   bless
> With more love,
>   not less.[4]

This way of blessing is not an easy way. *Chet*'s is not an easy path. It takes time to ripen into the wisdom, *chochmah* (another *Chet* word), of embodying this attitude toward life and fear. Many Jewish holidays last for eight days, suggesting that a period of time is required before we pass through the gateway and reach completion. Transformation doesn't usually happen all at once.

The eight days of *Chanukah*, for example, honor the cycling of time at the winter solstice and recall the miracle of one day's worth of oil lasting for eight. By eating and living in humble *sukkot*, huts, for the eight days of *Sukkot*, we remember the forty years that the Jews dwelt in huts during their sojourn in the Sinai. In the Diaspora, Passover is observed for eight days to commemorate the escape from Egypt and the Hebrews' long years of wandering in the desert. By lasting for eight days, these holidays allow us to deepen into sacred time and to feel more deeply how our ancestors struggled through the challenges of life.

As celebrated in Israel, the eighth day of *Sukkot* is known as both *Shemini Atzeret*, "Retreat of the Eighth Day," and *Simchat Torah*, "Rejoicing with the Torah." (In the Diaspora, these holidays are celebrated on two separate days.) With the harvest complete, *Shemini Atzeret* marks the traditional day for praying for rain to help the next season's harvest. *Simchat Torah* celebrates the completion of the annual cycle of readings of the Torah and the beginning of the next cycle. Both are *Chet*-powered holidays in that they celebrate endings and the jumping off into the unknown, into the *Chet*, infinity, of new beginnings once again.

Rebbe Nachman actually encouraged literal jumping on *Simchat Torah*. He taught that on this day people should dance and turn somersaults and leap off the ground in an effort to defy gravity and transcend the limitations of the physical world. Rabbi Aryeh Kaplan writes that when we dance with the Torah on *Simchat Torah*, "we are expressing the fact that on this day we are able to transcend the physical...going beyond any barriers and boundaries that were thought to be impossible to overcome."[5]

This is the *chutzpah* of *Chet*: to jump out into the infinite, into the unknown, beyond the barriers that seem to hold us back!

Chet's Shadow

To feel that "all of this world is a very narrow bridge," as Rebbe Nachman put it, can be overwhelming. We can become paralyzed with fear, unable to move along the bridge at all, or panicked by fear, acting wildly and dangerously. The challenge of *Chet* is to make fear an ally, so that, rather than a drain and a terror, it connects us more deeply to life and becomes a source of energy.

We have seen how *Chet* is a sign of *chadash*, the new. While freshness and innovation are wonderful, it's easy to become addicted to newness. Do we constantly crave novelty? Are we never satisfied? Do we disparage or wantonly deconstruct the time-honored and venerable? New doesn't always mean "improved." On the contrary, what has stood the test of time may often be more sound and have more integrity than the latest invention.

Chet is the first letter of *cheit*. Usually translated as "sin," *cheit* literally means "to miss the mark." *Chet*'s impulsivity may need to be tempered, and we may be well-advised to aim a little better before making a leap. *Cheit* is also a reminder of the negative aspects of *chutzpah*, such as arrogance and rudeness.

Personal Comments

At the wedding of my friends, Rabbi Aryeh called me under the canopy to offer a blessing. I had been sitting just a few feet away from the *chupah*, but as soon as I walked underneath it, I felt I had just come within an invisible but extraordinarily powerful force field. The feeling reminded me of the time I entered the sacred arbor during a Lakota Sun Dance. When I myself was married a few weeks after my friends' wedding, I found the *chupah* to be a magical, alchemical container.

Chet is the *chupah*. *Chet* sets up a transformational force field. Within that force field miracles happen. By the time we emerge through the gateway of *Chet*, our lives will have been deepened and enlivened. *L'chayim*!

Summary for Chet

Numerical value:	8
Meanings:	Life. Fear. Grace. *Chutzpah.*
Application:	Move to a higher level, taking things to a new octave.
	Pass through a gateway to new beginnings.
	Feel the fear and do it anyway.
Shadow:	Becoming incapacitated by fear.
	Always craving the new.
	Indulging in arrogance, rudeness, pushiness.
Reflection:	What metaphorical *chupah* am I entering into, standing within, or emerging from?
Suggested action:	Do something today that takes some *chutzpah.*

CHAPTER NINE

TET

(teht)

SOUND: *t*

NUMERICAL VALUE: 9

Meanings

The Talmud teaches that it is a good sign when the letter *Tet* shows up in a dream because the first *Tet* in the Torah appears in the word טוב, *tov*, "good": "God saw that the light was good."[1] *Tet* symbolizes essential, fundamental goodness.

Tet is a symbol of the primal energy of the feminine. The letter takes the form of a snake coiled in on itself. For centuries before the serpent became associated with evil, it was a representation of the divine feminine. *Tet's* shape suggests a vase or a cup, symbols for the womb. As the ninth letter and the number nine, *Tet* holds the rhythm of the nine months of pregnancy. This letter of goodness contains the power of gestation and the potential of life.

At the same time, Kabbalists associate *Tet* with a key image of masculine potency, the rod or the staff, because it is the final letter of the Hebrew word for "rod," שבט, *shevet*, and the central letter of "staff," מטה, *mateh*. Staffs and serpents are closely linked to each other in folklore and imagery. Moses casts down his staff and it becomes a serpent. Then, he picks up the serpent and it becomes a staff once again.[2] A curious incident occurs during the Israelites' wandering in the desert. To protect the people from poisonous snakes who bit and killed them, Moses, in shamanic fashion, builds a copper image of a snake and sets it on a pole. When people are bitten, they look upon this copper serpent and are healed.[3]

The image of two snakes or a double-headed snake entwined around a staff is an ancient one, predating the Israelites. It symbolizes the potent mingling of the masculine and the feminine, and is considered life-giving and healing. The image survives to this day as the caduceus, the wand of Hermes. The Seal of Aesclepius, the sign of the medical profession, consists of a similar image, that of a single snake wrapped around a staff. *Tet* is a kind of caduceus or Seal of Aesclepius in letter form.

However, *Tet* is also linked with death. Kings marked burial places with the sign of *Tet*. In several languages, the word for death sounds similar to *Tet* (which some pronounce "teth"), such as the English word "death" and the German *tot*.

This letter is associated with *teet*, the Hebrew word for "mud." Mud is the matrix of both death and life. All beings return to the earth when they die, absorbed back into the mud. But mud is also primal matter, or *mater*, Mother Nature, the origin of life, from which creation sprouts.

Tet, therefore, represents the procreating, the gestating, the flowering, and the decaying of all things. *Tet* teaches that all of this, this endless cycle of life and death, is *tov*, good.

Application

As *Chet*, the previous letter of the *Aleph Beit*, carries the energy of marriage through its form as the *chupah*, the wedding canopy, this ninth letter, *Tet*, contains the next phase of life: the power of conception and pregnancy, both literally and metaphorically. *Tet* is central to the Hebrew word for bed, *mitah*. Beds are the locus of procreation, where the male unites with the female to create new life. *Tet* is a sign of new creation. When *Tet* appears in our hands, good questions to ask are: What new life is growing inside me? On what level and with what am I "pregnant"? What is hidden, gestating, getting ready to be born?

Pregnant women often feel the instinct to nest, to retreat and protect the new life growing within. Choosing *Tet* offers an opportunity to quietly cherish and nurture a new idea or project, letting it gradually mature inwardly before exposing it to the sometimes harsh outside world.

Tet may also indicate a stage of shedding, the way a snake sheds its skin. What have we outgrown, what do we need to let go of, let die, in order to make way for new life?

Tet may represent a period of quiet reflection and protection. A snake is very vulnerable after it has shed its old skin and before its new one has toughened. It's a time to lay low and avoid danger.

The *tov* of *Tet* is a deep, profound, inner goodness, the primal goodness of creation, independent of circumstances. Two brothers once asked the Hasidic leader, the Maggid of Mezritch, how it was possible to bless God equally for both the good and the bad. The Maggid told them to visit his student Reb Zusya to find the answer. Reb Zusya was terribly poor and pain-ridden, but when the brothers found him and asked him their question, he was perplexed. "I don't know why the Maggid sent you to see me. I've never had a bad day in my life."[4]

In like mode, Zen Master Yun-Men addressed his assembly, "I don't ask you about the fifteenth day; come, give me a word about after the fifteenth." The fifteenth day is the day of the full moon, which symbolizes completion or enlightenment. Yun-Men is asking, in other words, "Don't tell me about the state of enlightenment, when everything is complete and full. What do you have to say about after enlightenment?" None of his students could respond, so, answering his own question, Yun-Men replied, "Every day is a good day."

Yun-Men's pronouncement is easy to misunderstand or trivialize. Like Reb Zusya, Yun-Men is speaking at the level of essential, fundamental reality. These two teachers are not sugar-coating suffering.

They are not, like Dr. Pangloss in Voltaire's *Candide*, pontificating that everything happens for the best in this best of all possible worlds.

Yun-Men's words, resonating through the centuries, form the basis of a famous Zen *koan*. *Koans* are not inexplicable puzzles; they are direct, cogent presentations of fundamental reality. They represent essential themes of life to be made clear. *Koans* are to be embodied, not merely speculated upon. How does one embody "every day is a good day"? This is the challenge of the Zen student as he or she takes up this *koan* with the master.

The challenge can't be met through naive, facile, pollyannish optimism. The goodness Reb Zusya and Yun-Men are expressing goes beyond superficial philosophizing to a direct experience of fundamental life. *Tet* challenges us to experience life at this profound, absolute level, where the essence of God's creation is the power of things as they are, a level at which "good" and "bad" cease to exist.

On the relative plane, on the other hand, where good and bad and all other dualities live, we must keep our eyes open to the reality of evil, act to weaken evil's force, and aspire to the highest good.

We have seen that *Tet* is key to the Hebrew words for "rod" and "staff," *shevet* and *mateh*. David sings of the power of the rod and the staff in a psalm infused with the energy of *Tet*, "Though I walk through a valley of deepest darkness, I fear no harm, for You are with me; Your rod and Your staff — they comfort me."[5] Even in the most dire of circumstances, this staff can dispel fear and help us experience that "every day is a good day." The letter *Tet*, which is shaped like a cup, reminds us that our cup runs over with blessings. Even if we can't see it now, goodness is growing within us and will soon be born into the world. "Only goodness (*tov*) and steadfast love shall pursue me all the days of my life."[6]

When *Tet* appears, this caduceus in letter form, it is a time to balance the masculine and feminine parts of ourselves and draw on their combined power. *Tet* is a potent letter that activates potential by helping us become pregnant with new inspiration and then helping to gestate this new seed or life until it is ready to emerge into the world. Then, God willing, in the fullness of time, we will look at our new creation, and, like the Holy One in the beginning, pronounce it טוב, *tov*, very good indeed.

Tet's Shadow

To truly understand and experience every day as a good day, without closing our eyes and hearts to the reality of pain and suffering, is a huge task. One danger of *Tet* is to apply "positive thinking" in a superficial fashion. "Oh, it's all for the good," we blithely say, denying parts of ourselves by adopting a cheerful philosophy. The word "pollyannish" comes from the ever-cheerful heroine of a sentimental nineteenth-century novel. What is dangerous about pollyannism is that it actually empowers the shadow to ultimately arise with more force, either from within or without.

Then, there is the danger of imposing this "positive thinking" onto others, blaming victims of illness or accident, for example, for not being positive enough in their attitudes and thus bringing their diseases or injuries upon themselves. It's easy to polarize experience, trying to stave off the harsh pains and confusions of life by trying hard to convince ourselves that everything really is fine. *Tet*, on the other hand, represents balance, not polarization, acceptance, not denial, groundedness, not fanaticism, awareness, not sentimentality. *Tet* doesn't avoid the grief of death even as it embraces new life.

Personal Comments

I had a friend, may he rest in peace, named Dr. Francesco Patricolo, an eccentric genius who, among other things, performed jazz rap poetry. In one of his pieces, Francesco sang, "In the Fifties, I was a Beatnik, an evolutionary Edsel. In the Sixties, I was a Hippie, an unused byproduct of the Industrial Revolution. In the Seventies, I was a Punk, a one-man band in a rogue bathtub. In the Eighties, I was a Yuppie, a stained glass window in a zoo. Now, in the Nineties, at the close of the Twentieth Century, I'm a Dumpy Grumpy."[7]

I sometimes feel like a Dumpy Grumpy myself. At those times, the world seems harsh, people look ugly, and everything appears bleak.

Tet has the power to break me out of a spell of gloom and negativity. *Tet* comforts me with a warm feeling. I feel safe within its shelter. Gradually, I become more aware of the good that underpins my life. Maybe today is a good day after all!

ט

Summary for Tet

Numerical value:	9
Meanings:	Goodness. Serpent. Staff. Mud.
Application:	Enjoy a time of conception and gestation.
	Shed what is outgrown and needs to be let go.
	Cultivate the creative power of the feminine and the potent power of the masculine.
Shadow:	Over-emphasizing "goodness."
	Pollyannish optimism; facile positive thinking.
Reflection:	What have I outgrown, what do I need to shed, to let go of, in order to make way for new life?
Suggested action:	Plant a seed. Then, protect and nurture it as it gestates and sprouts.

CHAPTER TEN

YUD

(yud rhymes with "should")

SOUND: *y*

NUMERICAL VALUE: 10

Meanings

Yud is the smallest letter of the *Aleph Beit*. Nonetheless, *Yud* has tremendous primal force and energy. *Yud* is a dynamo, a powerhouse. *Yud* shares the same Hebrew root as יד, *yad*, which means both "hand" and "power."

In fact, tiny *Yud* contains infinity. According to the Big Bang theory of the creation of the universe, all matter emerged from a tiny point that exploded outwards, expanding and gradually coalescing into galaxies and solar systems. *Yud* represents that beginning point, that small seed from which the whole creation sprouts.

Yud is the elemental, initiating force of life. The Hebrew root for *Yud* also means "to thrust." After the marriage of *Chet* and the conception and gestation of *Tet*, *Yud* thrusts its way into existence.

Yud is a cosmic letter. It's the only letter of the *Aleph Beit* that is suspended in midair, not grounded in the soil of this world.

The Talmud teaches that God used the letter *Hei* to create "This World," while the letter *Yud* was used to create "The World to Come."

72

In Hebrew grammar, *Yud* indicates the World to Come by denoting the future tense of verbs.

The primordial, initiating energy of *Yud* comes forth in some of the words it begins. *Yud* is the first letter of the most holy name of God, the יהוה, *Yud-Hei-Vav-Hei* (or YHVH). An abbreviation of YHVH, the honorific יי, usually read as *Adonai* and translated into English as "Lord," is spelled with two *Yud*'s. *Yud* begins another common name for the Divine, יה, *Yah*. It's also the first letter of the Jewish people, ישראל, *Yisrael*. This tiniest of letters sparks the mightiest of words.

Yud's power is also reflected in its number. *Yud* equals ten. Children learn to count on the ten fingers of their *yadayim*, hands. (As in English, the Hebrew word for hand, *yad*, also connotes "power," as in the phrase "the hand of God.") Ten is the basis of the decimal system. With ten songs, the Holy created the world. There are ten commandments or utterances, ten *sefirot* or branches on the Tree of Life, and ten people needed to constitute a prayer quorum or *minyan*. The holiest day in the Jewish calendar is *Yom Kippur*, the tenth day of the new year. The basic, powerful number of *Yud*, ten, is one root of our ability to measure existence.

Application

Yud carries us fast, on a powerful wave of transformation, into the future, into the world to come. One writer describes *Yud* as "a cosmic messenger bringing movement and change into our lives."[1] The word for "exodus," יציאה, *yetziyah*, begins with this letter. When *Yud* thrusts its way into our lives, we are being propelled, maybe willy-nilly, into a new level of experience. An exodus can be scary, exciting, tragic, promising. *Yud* shows that no matter how an exodus feels to us, it's impossible to hold on to the past. Life continually propels us into the unknown.

The powerful energy of *Yud* is concentrated in its small form. This letter, not much more than a point itself, encourages us to come to the point, to concentrate. How can we best focus our energies in order to ride *Yud*'s wave of transformation as gracefully as possible and arrive safely at a new location? That's little *Yud*'s big question. We may be called upon to prioritize, to let go of what is no longer needed, to become clear about what we truly want to carry with us into the future.

Yud is a letter of great force, yet, being so small, *Yud* is also the sign of humility. *Yud* is certainly not inflated, puffed up, ostentatious. Its power is contained, almost hidden. *Yud* is easy to underestimate. Moses, made shy by a speech impediment, and described in Torah as "very humble,"[2] nonetheless led a whole nation on an exodus out of slavery to freedom. Mount Sinai, where this modest man spoke directly with God and received Torah, was a relatively small, unimposing-looking mountain. Even the Hebrews were (and are) a small tribe. The Torah describes them as "among the smallest of all the nations."[3]

Smallness and humbleness don't impede greatness, however. *The Zohar* says, "Whoever humbles himself, God raises."[4] *Yud* calls us to humble ourselves, to loosen attachment to ego, but at the same time not to underestimate our tremendous power and potential for creativity and love and liberation.

Micah gives a prescription for acting in accord with *Yud*'s energy: "Do justly, love kindness, walk humbly with your God."[5] Moving through the world with this type of attitude is an exodus out of narrow egoism to expansive freedom.

A poem by the Sufi poet Rumi expresses the paradox embodied by *Yud*:

> I am so small I can barely be seen.
> How can this great love be inside of me?
> Look at your eyes. They are small,
> but they see enormous things.[6]

Having humility is more easily said than done, of course. Once, two wealthy businessmen were competing to show who was the most devout. After the lengthy synagogue services were over and everyone else had left, each remained in his place, continuing to pray. There they stayed, while the temple *shamash*, or custodian, swept and straightened up around them. Finally, one of the businessmen stood up and loudly proclaimed, "In the eyes of God, I am nothing!" and sat down.

Soon, the second businessman stood up and shouted, "In the eyes of God, I am nothing!" Then, he sat down.

The *shamash*, very impressed, had been watching this, and inspired, he too yelled, "In the eyes of God, I am nothing!"

The first businessman then turned to the second, pointed at the *shamash*, and whispered derisively, "Look who thinks he's nothing!"

Yud doesn't call for false modesty, affected humility. Rather, it challenges us to feel aligned with the grand sweep of cosmic energy thrusting us and the universe forward and outward into the future. Hang onto your seat. *Yud* is taking you on the ride of your life!

Yud's Shadow

As the only letter suspended in mid-air, *Yud* is the least grounded of the letters of the *Aleph Beit*. A danger of *Yud* is becoming un-grounded, or "spacing out." If we're focusing too much on the exodus, on moving into "the world to come," we may be missing what's right here before us. If we have our heads in the clouds, we may stumble on the rock in our path. We need to pay attention to the present, even as we move forward into the future.

The holy exodus that *Yud* embodies can become distorted and wind up as chronic displacement and restlessness. *Yud* calls us to move *toward* what we love instead of merely running away from what oppresses us.

Yud moves quickly and powerfully and brings these transformational qualities to our lives. Excessive and frenetic motion, however, can be upsetting or unhealthy. Sometimes change just grabs hold of us and we're off! But other times, through focused intention or action, we can temper the change, slow it down a little to a more manageable pace and scope. Change for its own sake is often not helpful. But change is inevitable. *Yud*'s challenge is to feel settled, even in the midst of change.

Personal Comments

"Where are we going?" a little rascal asks Stymie in the old "Our Gang" movie series as the kids careen downhill in a makeshift go-cart. "I don't know, brother, but we're on our way!" replies Stymie.

When *Yud* thrusts me forward, and the wind is whistling by my ears, and I know some radical change is taking place and in fact is picking up momentum, I think of Stymie. "We're on our way!" The World to Come is coming on fast. Humility arises naturally then as I realize I have no idea what's going to happen next. At times like that, I pray for grace and composure in the face of change, and I cry out to *Yah*, to *Yud-Hei*, for protection and guidance.

Summary for Yud

Numerical value:	10
Meanings:	Hand. Power. Thrust.
Application:	Align oneself with movement and change by clarifying priorities and letting go of what is no longer needed.
	"Do justly, love kindness, walk humbly with your God."
Shadow:	Becoming un-grounded, "spacing out."
	Fleeing.
	Excessive and frenetic motion.
Reflection:	How can I best focus my energies in order to ride *Yud*'s wave of transformation as gracefully as possible and arrive safely at a new location? Am I holding onto opinions and ego attachments that might impede *Yud*'s transformational power or make for a bumpier ride?
Suggested action:	What kind of future do you want? This very day, take a small step toward realizing it.

CHAPTER ELEVEN

KAF

(kahf)(final form: ך)

SOUND: *k*

NUMERICAL VALUE: 20

Meanings

As the first letter of כסא, *kisay*, "throne," and כתר, *keter*, "crown," and a key letter in *melech* and *malchah*, "king" and "queen," *Kaf* is a sign of royalty and majesty.

Keter is also the name of the highest *sefirah* or branch on the Tree of Life. Each *sefirah* reflects an aspect or energy of the Divine. *Keter* is the "crown of God," the realm that is closest to Heaven, beyond human comprehension.

The name of the lowest branch of the Tree of Life, מלכות, *Malchut*, "kingship" and "queenship," also contains *Kaf*. *Malchut* is the abode of the *Shechinah*, the feminine aspect of the Divine. It is the realm closest to our earthly, physical life.

Kaf, therefore, is connected to both the upper sphere and the lower. It is at once transcendent and the ground of being. *Kaf* is one of five letters that has a distinct form when it appears at the end of a word. The final form of *Kaf* extends below the line of writing, symbolizing the connection of the heavenly and the earthly, *Keter* and *Malchut*, spirit and matter.

As a word, *Kaf*, כף, means the palm of a hand (and the sole of a foot). Palms are associated with productive labor, as in the phrase "the toil of your palms." Palms represent the power to create or achieve.

Application

The characters in fairy tales, as in dreams, embody archetypes that point to qualities within each of us. Kings and queens are key figures in stories around the world. Sometimes in these tales princes or princesses wander lost in the world, unaware of or cut off from their royal heritage. They must undergo various trials and deepen in wisdom and life experience before they can reclaim their rightful place on the throne. The letter *Kaf* is the dream, the fairy tale, of inner kingship and queenship. *Kaf* calls us to claim, in our lives, more sovereignty and majesty.

William Stafford's poem "A Story That Could Be True" addresses this possibility:

> If you were exchanged in the cradle and
> your real mother died
> without telling the story
> then no one knows your name,
> and somewhere in the world
> your father is lost and needs you
> but you are far away.
> He can never find
> how true you are, how ready.
> When the great wind comes
> and the robberies of the rain
> you stand on the corner shivering.
> The people who go by—
> you wonder at their calm.
> They miss the whisper that runs
> any day in your mind, "Who are you really, wanderer?"—
> and the answer you have to give

no matter how dark and cold
the world around you is:
"Maybe I'm a king."[1]

"Maybe I'm a king." "Maybe I'm a queen." *Kaf* reminds us that, no matter our outward situation, we are each the king and queen of our experience. As *Keter* and *Malchut* are woven into the very fabric of existence as revealed by their commanding places in the Tree of Life, the inner *Keter* and *Malchut*, crown and kingdom/queendom, are inherent in our very natures.

How would one act if one were a king, a queen? With what dignity, responsibility, and assurance would one comport oneself and deal with others? When *Kaf* appears, it's an opportunity to act as if this were the case, not in a grandiose or arrogant fashion, not tyranically, but in a way that embodies the archetype of the noble, good king or queen. In myth and story, the good ruler restores order, health, creativity, and prosperity to the land. Embracing the power of *Kaf* can help bring these qualities into our lives.

"Majesty" is defined as sovereign power, authority or dignity, grandeur; greatness or splendor of quality or character. *Kaf* is a call to majesty, to splendor. The most influential book of Jewish mysticism is *The Zohar*, referred to in English as *The Book of Splendor*. "Splendor" here refers to the brilliance of the Divine, and also to the brilliance of its creation, including humans. To claim splendor is to claim our birthright as children of the Holy One.

Kaf, as "palm," beckons us to create something splendid in the world through the works of our hands. This creation can literally be the work of our hands, such as sewing, woodworking, pottery, cooking, or art or handicraft of any sort. And, of course, this creation can be the work of our hands in a metaphorical sense only. *Kaf*'s message is that each of us has a unique gift to offer, a brilliance that only we can bring into existence. Related to both "creation" and "crown," *Kaf* conveys the power to create a "crowning achievement," a noble accomplishment that helps manifest the kingdom and queendom of the Divine right here. To realize a crowning achievement, one must have a strong and focused intention, or *kavanah*, another word energized by *Kaf*.

For centuries, Jewish sages have taught that strong *kavanah* is essential for effective prayer and the fulfillment of sacred acts. Kabbalistic texts are filled with detailed instructions and practices for achieving transcendental states through focusing one's concentration.

Cultivating a clear, focused intention helps with the accomplishment of any act, however, not just "mystical" ones. The word *kavanah*, כוונה, comes from the root, *kiven*, כון, "to aim." *Kaf* calls us to aim thoughts and actions carefully, to best realize our goals. When we aim with conscious intent, we are much more likely to hit the mark. Determination, courage, perseverance, focused attention — all are qualities of *kavanah* which this letter *Kaf* evokes.

In various martial arts, such as tai chi and aikido, the student learns to focus and circulate *chi* or *ki*, the life energy and vital force of one's body and the universe. A Hebrew word for "strength" or "energy," כח, *koach*, begins with *Kaf*. Often, *koach* or *ki* is directed through the palms of the hands. Through its meaning as "palm," *Kaf* leads us to channel our own life energy with the clarity, control, and power of a martial artist. If we have become scattered or unfocused, *Kaf* is the *sensei*, the *rebbe*, the master, who helps reconnect us to the flow of *ki* in the *dojo*, the training center, of our life.

In this way, *Kaf* as *kavanah* and *Kaf* as "palm" unite to guide us toward greater mastery and power as we focus our intention and aim our life strength and energy toward a majestic goal.

Kaf's Shadow

Power is seductive. It easily corrupts. A king or queen may become a tyrant and a bully. As it calls us to greater power and majesty, *Kaf* has the potential to be abused. Arrogance, haughtiness, self-righteousness, manipulation are some of the pitfalls.

Will is a tricky matter. If we are not careful, strong and clear intention can quickly cross the boundary into destructive willfulness. Before we know it, we've become despots. A precaution against becoming trapped in this dynamic when working with the powerful energy of *Kaf* is to remember the simple prayer, "Not my will, but Yours be done."

Personal Comments

I move quickly toward Aki Fleshler, the aikido instructor, my hand raised as if to strike him. Suddenly, I find myself flying through the air. The next thing I know, I'm on the grass, lying on my back with the bemused instructor standing several steps away, eyeing me calmly. How'd he do that? It seemed as if he had hardly moved in response to my attack and yet here I am, undisputedly on the ground.

Sensei Fleshler was a master of *ki*. With subtle movements of his hands and body, and a powerful intention, he had been able to redirect my own energy to send me flying. The letter *Kaf* is the aikido master of the Hebrew alphabet. Grounded, intent, dignified, and powerful, *Kaf* is a letter you don't want to fool around with or underestimate. What a forceful ally, however, to have on your side! When *Kaf* is fully integrated into our being, we move with assurance through changing circumstances, in tune with the flowing *ki* of life.

כ
Summary for Kaf

Numerical value:	20
Meanings:	Palm (of the hand). *Melech*, king, and *Malchah*, queen. *Keter*, crown. *Kavanah*, intention.
Application:	Act as if one were a king or queen. Develop a strong and clear *kavanah*.
Shadow:	Becoming a tyrant. Arrogance and willfulness.
Reflection:	What is a unique gift I have to offer, a brilliance that only I can bring into existence? How can I best begin or continue to manifest that gift?
Suggested action:	For thirty minutes today, comport yourself as if you were a noble, courageous, good-hearted king or queen. And speak to others as if they too were kings and queens.

CHAPTER TWELVE

LAMED

(lah'mid)

SOUND: *l*

NUMERICAL VALUE: 30

Meanings

The Hebrew root for *Lamed*, למד, means both "to learn" and "to teach." It also represents a goad or a prod for guiding oxen or cattle.

As a prefix, *Lamed* means, among other prepositions, "to," "toward," "into," and "unto." *Lamed* indicates movement toward something.

It is also the first letter of לב, *lev*, heart.

Lamed is the tallest letter in the *Aleph Beit*. Traditionally described "a tower soaring in the air," *Lamed* ascends above the upper line of the script of all the other letters.

Application

If tall *Lamed*, this sign of an ox-goad, lifts its head into our sights, we ourselves may need to be goaded into movement. Is there some project or activity about which we could use a prodding? *Lamed* signifies a time for getting things going, for initiating action. If we have been procrastinating, *Lamed* is the goad that says, "All right! Time to get moving!"

Because *Lamed* is the first letter of *lev*, heart, this movement is aligned with our innermost being. Where is our passion and delight? Since, as a preposition, *Lamed* means "to" or "toward," this letter symbolizes aspiration, and the movement of the heart toward a goal or purpose, toward the heart's desire.

A student asked the Seer of Lublin to show him one universal way to the service of God. The great rabbi replied that it was impossible to tell people one specific way they should take to the service of God because there were so many ways and each person is so different. The Seer gave this advice, however: "Everyone should carefully observe what way their heart draws them to, and then choose this way with all their strength."[1]

Lamed prods us to carefully observe and then choose with all our strength. What's holding us back? Are we living out someone else's vision of what we might be or do, instead of following our own heart's urging?

Or is it uncertainty, despair, lack of confidence, fear that's making it hard to commit to a course of action?

Rumi writes,

> These
> spiritual window-shoppers,
> who idly ask, How much is that?
> Oh, I'm just looking...
>
> Even if you don't know
> what you want, buy something,
> to be part
> of the general exchange.
>
> Start a huge and foolish project,
> like Noah.
>
> It makes absolutely no
> difference what people
> think of you.[2]

When we are beset by ambivalence, procrastination, timidity, or confusion, by anything that inhibits appropriate action, *Lamed* encourages us. "Choose!" the letter prods. "Buy something!"

As the biggest letter of the *Aleph Beit*, *Lamed* encourages us to "think big," to start a *huge* project. Even if it appears foolish, we will undoubtedly learn from the experience. As Dan Millman writes in *The Way of the Peaceful Warrior*, "It's better to make a mistake with the full force of your being than to carefully avoid mistakes with a trembling spirit."[3]

Regrets about our lives more likely center on actions not taken than on active mistakes. Reb Zusya taught that after his death, in the next world he won't be asked, "Zusya, why weren't you more like Moses?" Instead, he'll be challenged, "Zusya, why weren't you more like Zusya?"

This is our challenge: to become fully ourselves, to be completely who we are, true to our core, our *lev*, not shrinking but standing tall in our own unique individuality, like the letter *Lamed*.

Life is the process of learning who we are and למד, *Lamed*, means "learning." Sometimes this learning takes place in a formal educational setting. Choosing this letter can indicate a propitious time to take a class, pursue a course of study, go back to school. But the setting doesn't really matter. *Lamed* reminds us that our job is to learn wherever we find ourselves, to be a student of life.

Lamed also means "to teach." Learning and teaching go hand in hand. Jewish tradition has always placed a great deal of value on both. The *melamed*, or children's teacher, has long been an honored position. In fact, the name of the heart of traditional Jewish study, the Talmud itself, תלמוד, comes from the root למד, *Lamed*.

Learning and teaching, to be most effective, must touch the *lev*, heart. *Lamed* cautions us against dry, cynical, abstracted learning, or dull, passionless teaching. Heart is what moves us, heart is what creates memorable teachers, and heart is what enables us to touch others.

Lamed, this letter of prodding, learning, teaching, aspiration, and heart, is the final letter of the final word in the Torah, *Yisrael*. It's a big letter and it carries great power. When we align ourselves with

Lamed's primal energy, we experience powerful lessons, learning who we are meant to be.

Lamed's Shadow

The prod of *Lamed* can get out of hand. We become driven, never satisfied, constantly goading ourselves or others or being goaded into more and more effort. Instead of fostering creativity and accomplishment, this drivenness can lead to workaholism and exhaustion, even madness.

If we focus *Lamed*'s energy of study and learning too narrowly on just bookish learning, we can become over-cerebral, divorced from the body and the natural world. Let's not forget kinesthetic, active learning, artistic learning, and the many other varieties of education that don't depend on books and words. When we remember that the word for "dance," *machol*, contains *Lamed*, the spirit of dance can inform our learning and save it from becoming dry and lifeless and out of balance.

"Thinking big" can easily become grandiosity and conceit. Egotism, more than the heart's aspiration, may drive a desire to stand out from the crowd, above it all, like tall *Lamed*. We may need to remember that, as E.F. Schumacher put it, "small is beautiful." The grand word, ישראל, *Yisrael*, after all, begins with the smallest letter of the *Aleph Beit* before ending with the biggest. Our magnificent ambitions may need to be tempered with some humility.

Personal Comments

An extraordinary storyteller lived in Boston, Massachusetts, named Brother Blue. During intermission at one of his performances, I went up to thank this venerable bard. Brother Blue was friendly and unpretentious. He asked me, "What do you do?" I was between jobs at the time and I hemmed and hawed and was starting to say what I used to do, when Brother Blue interrupted me. Fixing me with sharp eyes, he said forcefully, "What do you *want* to do?" Again, I hemmed and hawed, and finally he lowered his eyes and let me off the hook.

But the point had been made. The *Lamed*, the goad, of his re-mark struck home. What do I most want to do? What is my deepest passion? And what does the Holy want of me? What is my destiny? Frederick Buechner wrote, "The place God calls you to is the place where your deep gladness and the world's deep hunger meet."[4]

Brother Blue's words focused all these issues for me. His simple, yet powerful, question continues to urge me forward, helping me clarify my intention and move toward my heart's desire. *Lamed* prods each of us, "What do you want to do?"

ל

Summary for Lamed

Numerical value:	30
Meanings:	Goad, prod. Teaching. Learning. Heart. Aspiration.
Application:	Get moving.
	Think big.
	Learn and teach in accord with one's heart.
Shadow:	Grandiosity.
	Workaholism.
	Narrow bookishness.
Reflection:	What is my passion and delight, my heart's desire? What are some ways to move toward this desire?
Suggested action:	This very day, take the first steps toward accomplishing a project or task you've been putting off.

CHAPTER THIRTEEN

MEM

(mehm)(final form: ם)

SOUND: *m*

NUMERICAL VALUE: 40

Meanings

According to the *Sefer Yetzirah*, the seminal text of Hebrew letter mysticism, there are three Mother letters in the *Aleph Beit*, each of which represents a foundational element. א, *Aleph*, stands for air. ש, *Shin*, represents fire. מ, *Mem*, is the letter of water. The Hebrew word for water, מים, *mayim*, begins and ends with *Mem*. Many water words start with *Mem*, such as *mayahn*, "spring"; *mizraka*, "fountain"; and *motza*, "source." *Mem* represents the flowing, fluid rhythm of life.

In many languages, the words for "sea" and the "m" sound itself are related to the words for "mother." For example, in Hebrew, ים, *yahm*, means "sea," and אם, *aym*, means "mother." In French, *mer* means "sea" and *mère* means "mother." Water is the first mother. For nine months, a kind of eternity, we float in the salty seas of our mothers' wombs. "Mama" is one of the first words babies speak. "Mmm," grown-ups still say when something tastes good.

This Mother letter, *Mem*, embodies the mothering quality of compassion. The word for "womb," רחם, *rechem*, is the root of *rachamim*, "mercy" or "compassion." The Torah describes Thirteen Attributes of Mercy that were revealed to Moses on Mount Sinai. *Mem* is the thirteenth letter of the *Aleph Beit*. In many cultures, thirteen is a number of woman's power, as there are thirteen lunar and menstrual cycles in a solar year. The Thirteen Attributes of Mercy include kindness, generosity, tolerance, awareness, patience, compassion, and love.[1]

In the Hebrew numerical system, *Mem* equals forty, a number associated with purification. A traditional *mikveh*, the ceremonial bath of purification (most commonly used by Jewish women after completing their menstrual cycles), contains at least forty measures of rainwater. The Great Flood lasted for forty days and forty nights. משה, Moses (whose name, which starts with *Mem*, means "drawn from the water"), fasted and prayed for forty days during each of his three sojourns on Mt. Sinai to receive the Torah. The Hebrews wandered for forty years in the desert before being deemed ready to enter the promised land. Forty represents a washing clean, a cycle of purification.

The ultimate purification will be when the "knowledge of God covers the earth as the waters cover the sea."[2] Then, the world will be ready to receive, or embody the consciousness of משיח, *Mashiach*, the Messiah, whose name begins with the Mother letter, *Mem*.

Application

Each of us is naturally intimate with water. All of us floated in the womb waters prior to birth. Every day, water enters our mouths and courses through our bodies. Sixty-five percent of our bodies, in fact, consist of water. *Mem* is the letter that pours forth this sustaining, essential מים חיים, *mayim chayim*, the water of life.

When *Mem* flows into our lives, we are called to become like water, fluid, flexible, unstuck. *Mem* carries us along when we "go with the flow." This doesn't mean mindlessly or indulgently conforming to specific social expectations, or being totally passive. Rather, it means allowing ourselves to be borne on the river of life in a natural, organic way.

Part of the flow of life is the stream of emotions. Are there places in our emotional lives where we are stuck, where there's a logjam? *Mem* encourages us to search for ways to allow our emotions to flow once again. Are we attempting to hold back a flood of grief by becoming emotionally frozen or numb?

The word for "tumor" in the Mayan highlands of Guatemala translates as "solidified sorrow." The Mayans believe that if people don't grieve adequately, which includes, but is not limited to, freeing the flow of tears, sorrow then hardens and causes physical and emotional problems. The solution is to find safe ways to loosen tears so that the sad emotions can become liquid once again and pass through and out of the body instead of becoming stuck inside.[3]

Mem encourages us to nourish life with our tears so that happiness can sprout forth once more. Rebbe Nachman of Breslav writes, "How very good it is when you can awaken your heart and plead to God until tears stream from your eyes, and you stand like a little child crying to its parent."[4]

In the Grimm Brothers' tale of "The Water of Life," a king lies dying, and the only way he can recover is if someone can find and retrieve the Water of Life. One by one, the king's three sons head out on a quest to find this precious water. The youngest son eventually succeeds in gaining entrance to an enchanted castle. Yet, before he can locate the fountain from which springs the Water of Life, he must pass through a large hall full of men who have turned to stone, earlier seekers who got stuck and frozen.

In his commentary on this story, Michael Meade writes that living in this age "is like walking through a great weeping. It is like an ongoing funeral, a huge shedding of the life of the world...When the heart knows sorrow and never weeps, the sorrow gets locked like a storm inside the heart. When the storm can't pour out, it turns solemn, it becomes a stone weight. Grieving clears the heart and keeps it open."[5]

In order to find the sacred water that restores life to the kingdom, we must be able to bear the knowledge of death and loss without turning to stone. Grieving, in its various forms, enables us to do this.

Grieving is one form of purification. The *mikveh*, the ritual bath, is another kind of purification. When *Mem* shows up, it's time for a literal or figurative *mikveh*, immersing oneself in the rejuvenating and cleansing *mayim chayim*, waters of life. This can be a literal *mikveh* or a figurative one, such as the renewal of a solitary walk in the forest. The key is to wash away old accretions in order to be born afresh.

Mem invites us to examine ourselves and see what is not flowing in accord with our deepest desires, and then to reaffirm our intention to live in accord with these desires. *Mem*'s purifying influence inspires us to embody more fully and consistently the Thirteen Attributes of Mercy. As we express compassion, kindness, patience, we harmonize with the mothering energy of *Mem*.

מרים, Miriam, whose name begins and ends with *Mem*, embodies many qualities of this letter. Miriam helps save her baby brother, Moses, when he is cast into the river to avoid Pharaoh's decree that all Hebrew boy babies must be killed. She is also a noted midwife. After passing through the waters of the Red Sea, Miriam leads the Hebrew women in song and dance. The water from Miriam's well, and the *manna* (another *Mem* word), enable the Hebrews to survive during their forty years of wandering in the desert.

Selecting *Mem* may also indicate a time to refresh the flow of currency through one's life. If money and sustenance do not seem to be circulating adequately for us, what can we do to un-dam the current and let it flow more fully and freely down from the holy mountains where the snows of abundance gather?

One practical strategy for increasing the flow of abundance in our lives is to remember to be grateful. *Mem* as the letter, the sign, of Miriam, leads us to sing and praise the holy mystery for our survival up to this point. We've made it through some deep waters. Our struggles aren't over yet, but we're still alive! *Mem* also reminds us that deep wells exist of which we may not be aware. Hidden, ancient underground streams fill these wells. When we find them and dip our buckets, we tap into those deep currents of life. The old, old flow of *mayim chayim* then sustains us even as we proceed through the *midbar*, the wilderness and the desert.

Mem's Shadow

The Torah speaks not just of *mayim chayim*, but of "evil waters" that symbolize destructive or hurtful passions. Torrents of feelings may overwhelm us, washing away a sense of right and wrong. We may be flooded by big emotions. The challenge of *Mem* is to swim in the watery realms of emotion without drowning in them, and without losing sight of the solid ground of morality.

Another danger of *Mem* is to hang onto our sorrow as a mark of honor or a source of identity instead of releasing our tears and metabolizing them into some form of creativity as an offering to the earth and to the Holy. When we can offer up and transform our tears in this way, they nurture new life and prepare the ground for new blessings to grow.

Personal Comments

I'm in a Lakota sweat lodge. Pitch black. Extraordinarily hot. Sweat is streaming off me onto the cedar shavings covering the ground. Although all the ceremonial songs up to that point have been in the Lakota language, the leader surprisingly begins a song in English and Hebrew. "Draw water in joy from the living well. Draw water in joy from the living well. *Mayim chayim*, waters of life, *shalom*."[6]

How strange and beautiful to hear the Hebrew words from Isaiah in this Native American context. When the door of the lodge opens at the end of that prayer round, a bucket of water is brought in. Before we each drink a dipper of the precious water of life, the leader pours a little of it onto the hot rocks in the center of the lodge as an offering. "*Mini wakan*," he says in Lakota, "*Mini wa chozen*." "Water is sacred, water is life." After being so hot and sweating so much, we draw the water out of the bucket and drink it with joy indeed. The leader teaches that water is medicine; it is holy. To my thirsty and sweaty body at that moment, this is obvious and delightful fact, not just theory or fancy sentiment.

Out in the world, the letter *Mem* continues to remind me *mini wakan, mini wa chozen*. מים קדוש מים חיים, *Mayim kadosh, mayim chayim*. Water is sacred, water is life.

מ
Summary for Mem

Numerical value:	40
Meanings:	Water. Womb. Mercy.
Application:	Express compassion.
	Let tears flow and let sorrow be metabolized into creativity.
	Aspire to be fluid and flexible.
Shadow:	Becoming flooded by destructive passions.
	Drowning in sorrow.
Reflection:	Are there places in my emotional life where I am stuck, where there's a logjam? What are some ways I can free my emotions to flow more fluidly?
Suggested action:	Within the next seven days, experience some type of *mikveh*. This could range from a full-fledged formal *mikveh* to a quick dip in a stream or lake or even your own bathtub. Most important is to have an intention of purification as you immerse yourself. Afterwards, enjoy a simple cup of water.

CHAPTER FOURTEEN

NUN

(the vowel sound in *Nun* rhymes
with the vowel sound of "should.")

(final form: ן)

SOUND: *n*

NUMERICAL VALUE: 50

Meanings

In the order of the *Aleph Beit*, after *Mem*, the letter of water, comes *Nun*. In Aramaic, the ancient Semitic language closely related to Hebrew, the word נוּן, *nun*, means "fish."

The great fish that swallowed Jonah is a famous *nun* of the Bible. Jonah, with the letter *Nun* central to his name, had disobeyed the will of God. He wound up being cast overboard and then spending three days in the belly of the fish. In the midst of the giant *nun*, instead of death he found life, instead of destruction, renewal. Jonah emerged from his ordeal alive and transformed (although he still had lessons yet to learn about compassion and forgiveness).

Nun as "fish" also represents fertility and productiveness. Fish reproduce relatively quickly. In Genesis, fish were the first creatures to be blessed, "Be fruitful and multiply, and fill the waters in the seas."[1] Fish also make good fertilizer, helping crops become more productive. *Nun* is related to the root of the Hebrew words for "to sprout," *nav*, and "to flourish" or "to blossom," *n'nun*.

But, in the paradoxical way of many of the Hebrew letters, *Nun* also signifies the opposite of sprouting and flourishing, as it is related to נון, the root of the Hebrew words for "decline" and "degenerate." *Nun* encompasses both creation and destruction, ebb and flow. Like fish swimming amid the changing tides of the sea, *Nun* is at home in the changing circumstances of life.

Nun represents the number fifty. After a cycle of seven times seven sabbatical years comes the Jubilee, *Yovel*, the fiftieth year. (See chapter 7, *Zayin*, for more information on sabbatical years.) During the Jubilee year, slaves are freed, debts are forgiven, and land returns to its original owner. The Jubilee is a period of freedom and liberation and return.

In *Kabbalah*, fifty is also the number of the "gates of understanding." The fifty gates correspond to the fifty days of the *Omer* (literally a measure of wheat), the period between Passover and *Shavuot*. Passover commemorates the escape from enslavement in Egypt, and *Shavuot* celebrates the transmission of the Torah to Moses on Mt. Sinai. *Nun* marks the process of breaking out of bondage and moving toward revelation and home.

Jubilee, *Yovel*, literally means "the horn of a ram." It is the sound of the rams' horns that helps destroy the walls of Jericho. The person who leads the Hebrews in that battle is Joshua, referred to throughout the Torah as "Joshua, son of *Nun*." After Moses dies, the son of *Nun* is the one to finally lead the people into their promised homeland.

Application

Just as Joshua brought down the walls of Jericho, so too does *Nun* break down walls in our lives. Both self-imposed and externally-imposed limitations fall before the power of *Nun*. Many types of walls exist: hatred, fear, prejudice, ignorance. *Nun* brings encouragement that these walls can come tumbling down. Like Jonah, we can find life and hope in an apparently hopeless situation.

But, as in the case of Jonah, resurrection demands a radical transformation on our part. Something has to die for new life to come forth. After surviving in the belly of the beast, we can't just go back to business as usual. *Nun* challenges us to live as if we had emerged from the depths, miraculously brought back to life, cherishing what is truly important and letting go of outmoded self-concepts and old, negative patterns of thinking and acting.

Nun breaks through constrictions and breaks down barriers and leads us to a jubilee of emancipation. *Nun* sings, in the words of the Negro spiritual and the famous "I have a dream" speech of Dr. Martin Luther King Jr., "Free at last! Free at last! Thank God almighty, we are free at last!" This is the dream of *Nun*.

One way to make real the dream of freedom is suggested by the day-by-day process of counting the *Omer*. This symbolically and metaphysically retraces the passage of the Jews from their newfound escape from slavery to the profound revelation of the Divine through the Torah. This passage is a gradual, step-by-step journey. It has many moments of doubt, of backsliding and fear. We need discipline and perseverance to travel from bondage to enlightenment. *Nun* leads us on the path of liberation from whatever is constricting and oppressive, and encourages us, "Keep walking! The Promised Land lies ahead."

When counting the *Omer*, one enumerates, "Today is the (nth) day of the *Omer*." For Kabbalists, each day of the *Omer* corresponds to a different combination of qualities of the Sefirot, the branches of the Tree of Life. One meditates upon and seeks to embody the particular qualities of that day. The Fifty Gates of Understanding cannot be passed through all at once; it's a gradual, life-long, process. In fact, if one passes through the fiftieth gate, one has passed beyond our current plane of existence.

At the same time, when the walls of delusion fall, they fall! Enlightenment comes suddenly, provoked by a sound, a sight, a word, a smell. The world rushes forward, separations and barriers vanish, and step-by-step, day-by-day counting or practice falls completely away. The Promised Land is right here! Part of the tension, the dialectic, of *Nun* is between sudden liberation and daily discipline.

How do we handle the awesome responsibility of freedom? The escaped slaves, the Hebrews, receive the Ten Utterances and the Torah to help them. Freedom doesn't mean we can do whatever we want. Our behavior is circumscribed within an ethical framework.

After receiving the Torah, the Hebrews spend forty more years of wandering before they settle down. After revelation, life continues, step by step, day by day. This, then, is the true stuff of our freedom: eating, sleeping, walking, working, playing, praying, talking, singing. The road to the Promised Land *is* the Promised Land.

In Robert Louis Stevenson's fable "The Poor Thing," a poor fisherman proposes marriage to the daughter of a wealthy nobleman by saying, "Come, behold a vision of our children, the busy hearth, and the white heads. And let that suffice, for it is all God offers."[2] Common, everyday life is itself the great treasure. "Free at last!" sings the old spiritual. *Nun* begins and ends ניגון, *niggun*, the Hebrew word for "tune" or "melody." We could say that *niggunim* are "Jewish spirituals." These wordless hymns are intended to break down walls between the human and the Divine, to carry the singer up to ecstatic heights, to open the gates of heaven themselves. When *Nun* swims into our lives, it's a good time to learn and sing some *niggunim*. They open our hearts and lift our spirits and help walls come falling down.

Nun's Shadow

Fish are cold and fish are elusive. If we embody *Nun* too literally, we may try to avoid people by heading underwater, by diving deep out of sight. Not wanting to be caught, we can wind up swimming in lonely waters. Trying to be free, we can wind up trapped within self-imposed caverns. *Nun* challenges us to find a healthy balance of freedom and discipline, of spontaneity and practice, of ebb and flow. If we grasp too hard at just one of these dichotomies, we find ourselves snared on the line of dualistic thinking.

Personal Comment

At the old Koko An Zen Center in Honolulu, there was an inscription on the *han*, the wooden block that is struck to signal time: "Like a fish, like a fool." This describes a certain kind of freedom, a lack of self-consciousness, a total immersion in the moment that is lauded in Zen. *Nun* symbolizes this freedom, that of a fish swimming in water or a bird flying through air, naturally at home in the medium of their lives. *Nun* doesn't care for cleverness or good ideas. *Nun* doesn't care whether I "succeed" or "fail" at something. When *Nun* shows up, I remind myself, "Become more foolish, and more foolish yet. Be like a fish, like a fool!"

נ

Summary for Nun

Numerical value:	50.
Meanings:	Fish. Fertility. Growth and decline, descent and resurrection. Jubilee.
Application:	Swim, at home amid the ebbing and flowing currents of life.
	Break down walls of separation, ignorance, fear, hatred.
	Enjoy a *jubilee* of freedom.
Shadow:	Coldness.
	Aloofness.
Reflection:	Am I clinging to any outmoded self-concepts and old, negative patterns of thinking and acting? How can I let go of these and swim more freely in the currents of my life?
Suggested action:	Lift your heart and spirit by singing a *niggun* for at least five minutes today. If you don't know a *niggun*, find someone who can teach you, or seek some out online, or make up one, singing "*dai, dai, dai*" to your own tune.

CHAPTER FIFTEEN

SAMECH

(sah'mech)

SOUND: *s*

NUMERICAL VALUE: 60

Meanings

The name of the letter *Samech* is related to the Hebrew root סמך, "support" or "prop." *Samech* is the sign of divine support and protection. The ongoing nature of this support is embodied in the unbroken shape of the letter — it has no beginning or end. Its script form is a perfect circle.

The inside of the *Samech* is hidden, shielded. *Samech* initiates *sohirah*, the Hebrew word for "shield" and "buckler." The Psalmist sings that the truth of the Divine "shall be your shield and buckler."[1]

The סכה *sukkah*, or hut, which also starts with *Samech*, is a literal form of shelter. Other less physical sources of support that begin with this letter are: ספר, *sefer*, "book"; סדור, *siddur*, "prayer book"; and ספור, *sippur*, "story." Each of these can be a container or vessel of sustenance and protection.

The Hebrew root, *Samech*, means "to support" as well as "to be supported." *Samech* is thus a letter of interdependence, of mutuality.

Nothing exists in a vacuum or in isolation. Everything depends on everything else. We support even as we are supported.

Buddhists describe this vast web of connection as the Net of Indra. At each knot on this net is a unique jewel. Every individual jewel perfectly reflects all the other jewels in the net, and contains all the reflections within itself.

The English word for one type of jewel, sapphire, comes from the Hebrew, ספירה, *sefirah*. The *sefirot* are the vessels of divine energy in another model of existence, the Kabbalistic Tree of Life. *Samech* and the final form of *Mem* are the only two letters in the *Aleph Beit* that are completely enclosed. Like the jewels on the Net of Indra, each *sefirah* is completely unique and self-contained, whole unto itself, closed, and yet at the same time totally connected to the others. Also, each *sefirah* contains all the other *sefirot* within it.

While the self-enclosed nature of *Samech* makes this letter's energy hard to penetrate when threatened or attacked, it also can make it hard to penetrate, in the sense of being understood. *Samech* initiates the words *sod*, "secret," and *sodi*, "mysterious."

The Sefirot themselves are hard to understand. Traditionally, one was discouraged from even trying until one was married, at least forty years old, and had been formally accepted as a student by a *rebbe* who himself was qualified to impart these secret teachings. Their intensity was considered too great and potentially dangerous to be revealed to the uninitiated. Self-enclosed *Samech* is full of secret, contained power.

S'micha, סמיכה, ordination, starts and is ruled by *Samech*. Rabbis, cantors, *maggidim* or storytellers, preachers, healers, and judges all receive *s'micha*. It is an energetic empowerment directly transmitted from teacher to student.

Samech equals sixty. Solomon had a bodyguard of sixty heroes, valiant men who guarded him while he slept. "There is Solomon's couch, encircled by sixty warriors of Israel, all of them trained in warfare, skilled in battle, each with sword on thigh because of terror by night."[2] *Samech* as sixty encircles each of us within its protective force-field.

Application

The tension of *Samech* is between interdependence and independence, supportiveness and secrecy. When *Samech* circles into our lives, we confront this twofold nature. *Samech* challenges us to find a balance between these two tendencies. Now we comfort, now we are comforted. Now we praise, now we are praised. Now we give, now we receive. To become stuck on one side or the other of this give-and-take disrupts *Samech*'s circular flow of energy.

The Book of Ecclesiastes says there is a time and a season for everything, for giving birth and for dying, for seeking and for losing, for keeping quiet and for speaking. When *Samech*, this sign of the prop, shows up, it's a time for propping something up or allowing ourselves to be propped up. What needs our support today? In what ways can we allow ourselves to be supported? What aspects of our nature would benefit from support?

It can be hard to open up enough to be able to receive support. *Samech*'s self-contained form illustrates the tendency to hole up or isolate oneself. We can try to hide within a shell, circle the wagons and barricade ourselves from the outside world, but it won't work. Sooner or later, the world breaks in, if only in the form of the water we drink, the air we breathe, the birdsong we hear. The chair supports us even as we slump all alone at the lonely table. Can we let go and enjoy the generous support the chair provides?

The Reverend Martin Luther King Jr. wrote that everyone is "caught in an inescapable network of mutuality, tied in a single garment of destiny."[3]

As one Zen teacher put it, "We are all members of the same nose-hole society."[4]

Samech challenges us to claim our place in this society, to open ourselves to our particular spot in the Net of Indra, to engage in the give and take, the intercourse of life.

As sometimes happens with sexual relations, however, we can give away too much. We can get wounded in unhealthy ways. We can lose our treasure. Besides being the sign of mutual support, *Samech* is also the sign of self-containment, shielding, protection. It is wise to guard carefully the jewels of our inner treasure. And also not to covet someone else's.

"Tell a wise person, or else keep silent, because the massman will mock it right away," writes Goethe.[5] *Samech* is the letter of *sodot*, secrets. When is it wise and prudent to be secretive, and when is it uptight and fearful? When is it most appropriate to be open and sharing, and when to be guarded and shielded? There is a time and a season for everything, but sometimes it's hard to know what time it is right now!

Samech can support us in finding a healthy balance between these poles. The *Samech*-energy of the sixty valiant warriors who guarded King Solomon while he slept, swords at the ready, is also present to protect us. *Samech* protects by reminding us that there truly is nothing outside us. Walt Whitman wrote, "I am large. I contain multitudes."[6] Fundamentally, everything is contained within the primal circle of *Samech*. We are safe.

Samech's Shadow

One aspect of *Samech*'s shadow has already been mentioned — the tendency to become blocked off and shut down. *Samech* is a letter of protection, but it's easy to become overly guarded and excessively defensive. We may want to come out of seclusion and join the *hora*, the circular dance, of community.

Samech can also hold the twin pitfalls of becoming either too supportive or too dependent on other people. We can over-extend, going beyond what is healthy for ourself or others. On the other hand, we can lose sight of our own intact and contained nature, and become excessively dependent on someone else. When we find ourselves lost in either extreme, we can take ourselves in hand and be quiet within the *sukkah*, the shelter of our own unique, interconnected, mysterious self. There, our treasure waits for us.

Personal Comments

Our Passover *seder* was just about to end, and we wanted to sing one last song. Deborah thought of a good one, a modern chant in English that was easy to learn. "We are a circle within a circle, with no beginning, and never-ending." That was it. The whole song. The last line circled back into the first such that the song just kept going and going, building power as people's voices grew more confident, and becoming more rich as harmonies were added. Finally, after a long, almost ecstatic, time, the chant wound down and our *seder* was over. Our circle was complete.

Samech (which begins the word סדר, *seder*), represents this circle within a circle. The Passover *seder* itself circles back to our ancestors as we commemorate their struggles for liberation. *Samech* reminds me that, like Ezekiel's vision of a wheel within a wheel, I am part of circles within circles within circles within circles. All these circles have the power to spin me out of self-centeredness, at least for a little while, and remind me of the *sod*, the mysterious nature of our interconnectedness.

ס
Summary for Samech

Numerical value:	60.
Meanings:	To support. To be supported. Prop. Secret.
Application:	Find a balance between interdependence and independence, supportiveness and secrecy.
Shadow:	Becoming blocked off and shut down.
	Becoming either too supportive of or too dependent on others.
Reflection:	Who or what needs my succor? What kind of nurturance or assistance do I need?
Suggested action:	In a tangible way today, support someone else and allow yourself to be supported.

CHAPTER SIXTEEN

AYIN

(i'yin)

SOUND: silent[1]

NUMERICAL VALUE: 70

Meanings

Ayin, עין, means "eye," and its name sounds like this English word. *Ayin* represents various types of seeing such as insight, foresight, outlook, and perspective.

Eyes need light in order to see. *Ayin*, therefore, is a letter of light and enlightenment, as well as of sight. "Where there is no vision, the people perish," says Proverbs.[2] A seer maintains a vision for the community, and thus helps keep life alive. *Ayin* is the see-er of the *Aleph Beit*.

This seer quality of *Ayin* is reinforced by its numerical value. *Ayin* equals seventy. Moses appointed seventy elders to be the "eyes of the community" and help him judge the people. These seventy became imbued with the power to prophesy, and in this way gained the perspective needed to judge wisely. The seventy elders became the model for the *Sanhedrin*, the highest religious/judicial court of Israel.[3]

Ayin also means "spring" or "source."

Application

"Open your eyes!" is *Ayin*'s fundamental challenge. To actually notice the things of this world, to truly see what is before us, is an awesome task. When our minds are so full of thoughts that we barely pay attention to what's in front of us, we are not really seeing. So, one way to apply the lesson of *Ayin* is to look more closely at the world. What are the subtle textures of the clouds, the shades of blue and gray in the sky? What color is this person's eyes? How do the trees sway in the breeze? As Yogi Berra said, "You can see a lot just by observing."

The Japanese poet Bashō wrote,

> When I look carefully —
> Nazuna is blooming
> Beneath the hedge.[4]

Nazuna is the small plant called "shepherd's purse" in English. It's easy to overlook or take for granted as just a weed, but on observing carefully, Bashō appreciates it profoundly. *Ayin* urges us to look with equal care on our surroundings in order to fully appreciate and not overlook life.

At the same time, *Ayin*, as the letter of insight, leads us to look within, to gaze beyond surface appearances to the inner workings of a situation, to see all the way to the *Ayin*, the "spring" or "source." As we sharpen our vision and develop the ability to see what is not apparent to the physical eye alone, we gain a deeper perspective. For example, we may become aware of words unspoken, of subtle emotions, of fears and desires and insecurities that underlie the behavior of others and ourselves. We develop, as we gain in insight, a more compassionate and less reactive outlook.

Without a spirit of compassion, the *Ayin* of insight can turn into *ayin hara*, the evil eye. This is the judgmental stare, the cold gaze, the jealous look, the hard eyes full of cursing. Rebbe Nachman said, "Take care, there is much power in a glance. If accompanied by a malicious thought, it can cause harm. This is what is known as the evil eye."[5]

Ayin's challenge is to be discerning without being demeaning, to let kindness temper the keenness of our sight, to keep our eyes open to evil and greed in the world, without becoming cynical or hopeless.

As the sign of the seventy judges Moses appointed, *Ayin* is a letter of wise judgment, of critical perception. When *Ayin* comes into our sights, it's a time to look carefully and evaluate clearly the matters before us, to deliberate as a distinguished judge might, over the facts of the situation, perhaps to view it in a different light. We need to watch out that we not be naively gullible and let someone pull the wool over our eyes, or permit ourselves to be hoodwinked by that which wishes us no good.

Also, we must be conscious of our own projections and prejudices which might skew our sight. Libra, as the image of impartial Law, wears a blindfold as she holds the scales of justice in her hands, in order that she may see and judge clearly and fairly.

Sometimes sight can get in the way of a deeper kind of seeing. Tiresias, the famous seer in Greek drama and legend, was blind. The renowned Hasidic rabbi Jacob Yitzhak, known as the Seer of Lublin, was said to have very poor eyesight. *Ayin* is a letter of intuition, of inner sight and foresight, as much as literal seeing. Choosing this letter is a call to acknowledge and trust our intuition, to pay attention to our dreams. A prophet is clairvoyant, from the French word for "clear-seeing." *Ayin* calls us to cultivate such clear seeing, which may be latent and dormant within us. We begin by noticing and honoring intuitive feelings, and not reflexively dismissing them.

As the letter of light, *Ayin* sheds light on matters at hand. When *Ayin* shows up, it's time to illuminate some dark places, to gather information and insight. The time is ripe for enlightenment. Zen master Wu-men, writing in the thirteenth century, describes the experience of enlightenment as walking "hand in hand with all the Ancestral Teachers in the successive generations of our lineage — the hair of your eyebrows entangled with theirs, seeing with the same eyes, hearing with the same ears."[6]

The Christian mystic Meister Eckhart said, "The eye through which I see God is the same eye through which God sees me; my eye and God's eye are one eye, one seeing, one knowing, one love."[7] Realizing this intimate mutual seeing, when one sees God "eye to eye,"[8] is the ultimate aspiration of *Ayin*.

The "third eye" is the seat of wisdom in many Eastern cultures. This spot, on the forehead above and between the two eyes, is the location for the *tefillin*, the phylacteries worn during morning prayers. Choosing *Ayin* is an opportunity to pray that our third eye be opened, that we grow in wisdom and insight. "Open my eyes, that I may perceive the wonders of your teaching" is *Ayin*'s prayer.[9]

As we are able to look through the eyes of *Ayin*, we begin to make real the inspired vision of Joel: "Your sons and your daughters shall prophesy, your old men shall dream dreams, your young shall see visions."[10]

Ayin's Shadow

One shadow of *Ayin* manifests in a very literal way. When we are moving toward "the light," yearning for enlightenment, our shadow is behind us and we may be unaware of this dark side. The abuses of power and sex found in many religious communities is evidence of this tendency for seekers of the light to become blind to their own darker natures or to avert their eyes from seeing the faults of spiritual leaders. The Talmud cautions, "The greater the sage, the greater the evil inclination." *Ayin* demands clear yet compassionate vision and wise judgment of both ourselves and others.

Ayin is sometimes a symbol of coveting and greed. "The eyes of man are never satisfied," says Proverbs.[11] If we are prone to the "roaming eye," always trying to fill up with novel sights or new people, this letter can be a reminder to cultivate an inner seeing that does not grasp for satisfaction outside of oneself.

Personal Comments

The well-digger arrived at our rural property in his big truck loaded with pipes and winches and huge augers. He emerged from the large rig holding a small forked stick, a divining rod. The burly fellow then walked around the land, divining rod in hand, feeling for the subtle downward tug on the end of the stick that would indicate underground water and a propitious spot to sink a well. Finally, the signs were clear. At a certain spot, he said, two underground streams converged. Here was where the well should be located. He even accurately estimated the approximate depth at which we would hit water.

Shaped somewhat like a divining rod, the letter *Ayin* helps us divine, to foresee, by looking beneath the surface of things and finding underground currents of thoughts or emotions or energies. Its very name means "source" or "spring." When this letter appears, I remind myself to notice subtle tuggings of intuition. Insight deepens to the extent I can quiet my mind and allow *Ayin* to be my eyes, its ancient gaze penetrating to the heart of the matter.

ע
Summary for Ayin

Numerical value:	70
Meanings:	Eye. Insight. Vision. Spring or source.
Application:	Open our eyes.
	Look beyond the surface of things.
	Be discerning without being coldly judgmental.
	Cultivate intuition.
Shadow:	Blindness to the dark side of ourselves or others.
	Coveting and greed.
Reflection:	How can I strengthen my abilities of perception and deepen my intuition?
Suggested action:	For at least one hour today, practice expressing loving-kindness through your eyes, allowing them to communicate kindness and gentleness to those you encounter.

CHAPTER SEVENTEEN

PEH

(pay or peh)(final form: ף)

SOUND: *p, ph*

NUMERICAL VALUE: 80

Meanings

פה, *Peh*, means "mouth." It is the sign of the profoundly powerful activities of speaking and singing. In Genesis, the Holy creates the entire universe through these means.

Peh equals eighty. According to the Torah, Moses was eighty years old when he got the call to lead the Hebrews to freedom. Moses was able to speak with God "mouth to mouth"[1] and become God's spokesman despite having a serious speech impediment! (Some commentators say that Moses stuttered, while others believe he had difficulty enunciating specific consonants.)

When Moses beheld the vision of the burning bush and heard the Divine Voice telling him to lead the Hebrew people out of slavery in Egypt, he objected. Moses argued that he wasn't qualified to be the leader because he was "slow of speech, and of a slow tongue."

The Voice answered Moses' objections, "I will be with your mouth and teach you what to say." Furthermore, Moses' older brother Aaron would help as Moses' spokesman.[2] Moses is thus the prototype of one

who transcends limitations and whose mouth is freed to speak with
divine inspiration.

Application

Inspired speech or song is *Peh*'s ideal, where words flow with a spirit
of holiness, and we are able to say what is needed in an appropriate,
effective, and eloquent fashion. "The heart of the wise teaches his
mouth, and adds learning to his lips," is the word of Proverbs.[3] *Peh*
calls us to speak and sing from the heart.

"A person has joy by the answer of his [or her] mouth: and a word
spoken in due season, how good is it!"[4] Are there things that need to
be said? Is now the time to say them? *Peh* encourages us to speak out,
to speak up, to claim our right to be heard, and not be afraid.

On the other hand, in some situations, prudence and restraint
might be most appropriate. When *Peh* appears, it is an opportunity
to weigh our words. *Peh* can be a sign to be quiet, to close the mouth
and listen. Speech is extraordinarily powerful. It can be creative or
destructive. *Peh* reminds us to not underestimate this power. We
must especially be on guard that we not indulge in *lashon hara*, the
"evil tongue" of malicious gossip or slander.

"Right Speech" is one category of the Buddhist "Noble Eight-fold
Path" to calmness, insight, and enlightenment. Right Speech includes
refraining from telling lies, from creating disharmony through back-
biting and slander, from using malicious or abusive language, and
from foolishly babbling or gossiping. "When one abstains from these
forms of wrong and harmful speech one naturally has to speak the
truth, has to use words that are friendly and benevolent, pleasant
and gentle, meaningful and useful. One should not speak carelessly:
speech should be at the right time and place. If one cannot say something useful, one should keep 'noble silence.'"[5]

In a Hasidic tale, the prophet Elijah appears in disguise as a ragged
wanderer and reproaches Rabbi Bunam and his companions as they
debate the acceptability of the food being served them in a strange
inn. "Oh you Hasidim, you make a big to-do about what you put into

your mouths being clean, but you don't worry half as much about the purity of what comes out of your mouths!"[6]

Jesus similarly declared, "Not that which goes into the mouth defiles a person; but that which comes out of the mouth, this defiles a person."[7]

Sometimes, *not* speaking defiles a person. There are times when speaking is called for. Are we holding back from communicating our feelings or ideas out of timidity or shyness? Out of anger or resentment? *Peh* beckons us to speak when necessary and appropriate, to come forth as who we are and to not hide behind silence. We may have a "turning word" to share with someone, but it must be spoken for the turning to occur. Often, we regret things we failed to do or say more than the things we actually did or said. *Peh* urges, "Speak while you have the chance. Life passes quickly. Don't let that chance go by."

The attitude which underlies right speech is described by Robert Aitken in his appropriately titled book, *Encouraging Words*:

> Noble, upright speech arises from clear understanding that none of us will be here very long and it behooves us to be kind to one another while we can. It arises from knowing in our hearts that we need each other and cannot survive alone. I vow to speak out of consideration for the frailty of my friends, and my own frailty, and out of consideration for our intimate family relationship. I vow not to speak as though the errors of others were ingrained or as though I were separate.[8]

Before reading the *Amidah*, a core part of every Jewish prayer service, worshipers recite the following verse from Psalms: "Open up my lips, O Yah, that I may sing your praise."[9] This is *Peh*'s prayer: to have our lips be freed to express gratitude. Such gratitude, whether to the Divine or to other people or beings, needs to be expressed out loud. The Talmud teaches that feelings of friendship should be verbalized.[10] Similarly, repentance and confession are considered incomplete and ineffective until expressed aloud.[11] All sorts of pledges, from marriage vows to oaths of office, become official only after being spoken. *Peh* urges, "Speak!"

Spoken words are at the heart of Jewish religious observance. Each week, the Torah is chanted aloud. Silent reading of the Torah or other prayers is considered inadequate; the sound of the words must reverberate in the air to make the teachings come to life.

Speaking and hearing are profoundly intimate acts. "When I speak, the bones in your ear vibrate," said poet Etheridge Knight. *Peh* reminds us of the intimacy and power of the spoken or sung word, and encourages us to not take them for granted.

Instead, with awareness of the potency for good or ill of our words (or our silence), we can pray with David, "Let the words of my mouth and the meditations of my heart be acceptable in your sight, oh *Yah*."[12]

Peh's Shadow

Talking too much is one negative aspect of this sign of the mouth. "A fool's voice is known by multitude of words."[13] We may need continually to remind ourselves to exercise self-control and be quiet. This can be an ongoing practice.

Or, we may be too quiet. *Peh* calls us to balanced communication, to compassionate expression. Someone we know may desperately need a kind word spoken or a misunderstanding clarified.

The tendency to gossip, put people down, and spread rumors is all too human. *Peh* asks us to resist this temptation and instead to uplift our speech, to have our words be words of blessing, not cursing.

Personal Comments

It's natural for humans to talk, to sing, to tell stories. Sometimes, when I don't have to attend to the meaning of the words swirling around me, I can hear the human voices as sounds of the natural world, like birdsongs or cricket chirps or wind in the trees. In the multi-mouthed chorus of nature, humans' sounds are just one part of the mix.

When I can remember this way of perceiving human speech, I'm a little less likely to become upset or reactive because of someone's words. I also become less self-conscious and inhibited about sending my own voice out into the world. After all, it's just the sound of the earth expressing itself, the voice of nature coming through as my voice. *Peh* reminds me that the universe is full of many kinds of mouths and many kinds of speech. I pray that I am able to hear the harmony within this multitude of sound.

Summary for Peh

Numerical value:	80
Meanings:	Mouth. Communication.
Application:	Speak from the heart.
	Speak when needed and keep silent when appropriate.
	Practice "Right Speech."
	Express gratitude out loud.
Shadow:	Talking too much.
	Not talking enough.
	Gossiping.
Reflection:	Are there words I need to say to someone that I have been silencing out of fear or timidity or complacency? Is now the time to say them?
Suggested action:	For today, try to avoid gossiping, subtly or not so subtly putting people down, and all other negative speech.

CHAPTER EIGHTEEN

TZADI

(tsah'dee)(final form: ץ)

SOUND: *tz*

NUMERICAL VALUE: 90

Meanings

The name of this letter, *Tzadi*, צדי, or *Tzadik*, צדוק, is related to the Hebrew root for "just," "honest," and "righteous." This root denotes such qualities as devoutness, kindness, fairness, integrity. A *Tzadik*, a righteous one, helps sustain the universe through his or her virtue and good deeds. "The *Tzadik* is the foundation of the world," says Proverbs.[1]

Jewish tradition teaches that in every generation there are *Lamed-Vav Tzadikim*, "Thirty-six Righteous Ones," who hold the world together through their goodness and virtuous acts. These saintly characters are hidden, living humbly, and performing their wonderful and miraculous deeds in secret. Sometimes they are disguised as rough and unfriendly woodsmen, sometimes as beggars or simpletons. But no matter the outward form, the intention of a *Tzadik* is to uplift and unify.

Rabbi David Cooper writes, "Without the work of a *Lamed-vavnik*, the pain and suffering that would ensue would be unimaginable...It is the job of a *Lamed-vav Tzadik*…to constantly improve the destiny of those around him or her."[2]

A *Tzadik*, even when living all alone, hidden on the edges of society, serves and sustains the community and the world. Reflecting the fact that one cannot be a *Tzadik* in isolation, but only in relation to others, *Tzadi* is the first letter of many words related to groups and communities. For example, *tzibur* means "community" or "congregation," and *tzevet* means "team." Tzedakah is the word for "charity," the righteous action that connects people.

Tzadi is the central letter of מצוה, *mitzvah*. This word is often translated as "commandment" or "good deed" but the root meaning of *mitzvah* is "connect." *Mitzvot* connect us to the Holy One, to each other, and to all of creation.

ציצית, *tzitzit*, is another word powered by *Tzadi*. *Tzitzit* are the fringes on the four corners of a *talit*, or prayer shawl. Comprised of many individual threads woven together into strands, *tzitzit* symbolize the *Tzadi* power of connection. As Arthur Waskow puts it, "The *tzitzit* are, literally and visually, the Weave of Unity."[3]

Application

According to Jewish legend, the *Lamed-vav Tzadikim* usually live their lives and perform their noble deeds secretly. *Tzadi* reminds us to be alert to the presence of these Righteous Ones. If not for them, the world would collapse!

Who are these saintly characters who are the foundation of the world? Where are they? It's hard to know. Most of the time they remain hidden, in disguise, out of the limelight. Therefore, tradition teaches that we should regard everyone we meet as a possible *Tzadik*.

Rabbi Cooper writes, "A *Lamed-vav Tzadik* may hide in many disguises. The person giving us the hardest time may be saving our lives."[4] Elsewhere, he says, "Sometimes, for no reason at all, we go from a bad mood to a good mood; it could be the result of a *Lamed-vavnik* standing nearby. Indeed, sometimes we think we are having a casual conversation with a stranger, but in fact this other person is helping us avoid a serious tragedy."[5]

It is best, therefore, if we're not put off by surface appearances, but treat everyone with respect, as if the maintenance of the universe itself depends on this very person before us. How might the quality of our interactions improve if we were able to approach them with this attitude?

As we embody this perspective, we become more *Tzadik*-like, more righteous, ourselves. In our own unique ways, we can uplift our thoughts and actions and perform the deeds necessary to maintain and sustain the world. *Tzadi* challenges each of us to become a *Tzadik*.

When the letter *Tzadi* comes out of hiding and appears before us, it may indicate a time to serve a team or community or congregation in a more dedicated fashion, adding our energy to that of the group's. If we've kept ourselves aloof or separate, now can be a good time to reweave ourselves into the fabric of our neighborhood or family or group.

As the sign of *mitzvot* and *Tzedakah*, *Tzadi* also calls us to increase our performance of good deeds and our acts of charity, taking our expressions of generosity to higher levels.

The Talmud teaches that the best *Tzedakah* is given anonymously with neither the giver nor the receiver knowing the identity of the other.[6]

Mu-chou, a Chinese Zen teacher of the ninth century, fulfilled this ideal. Mu-chou lived by himself in a small hut near a road used by monks on pilgrimage. He would weave straw sandals of varying sizes and then secretly leave them by the side of the road. As they hiked down the road, monks would come upon this line of new sandals, find the right size, and continue on with gratitude. For years, no one knew who was making the sandals. Finally, Mu-chou's secret was discovered and he became known as the "Sandal Monk."[7]

A *Tzadik* sustains the world, is "the foundation of the world," but for most of us, the modern mode of living is not sustainable. In order to be *Tzadikim* in the contemporary industrialized world, we must learn and practice ways of living that strengthen the foundation of life and don't undermine or erode it further. Perhaps this means living simply and humbly like the legendary *Tzadikim* of the past.

Tzadi's Shadow

Self-righteousness is one of the pitfalls to watch out for when working with the energy of this letter of righteousness. Because *Tzadi* is formed by the letter *Nun* leaning down toward the left with the letter *Yud* resting on top of it, the rabbis of old taught that *Tzadi* represented the act of bowing down in humility. Remembering humility can temper the tendency toward getting puffed up with self-righteousness.

Another danger of *Tzadi* is to hold ourselves to unrealistically severe standards, to expect ourselves to be saints, and then to be harshly critical when we don't live up to this standard. This letter challenges us to live as much of a *Tzadik*-like life as possible while at the same time being gentle on ourselves. We're only human after all, not saints, and sometimes we find ourselves in complicated and confusing circumstances. Aspiring to be a *Tzadik*, but keeping a good-humored and forgiving attitude toward our own frailties and stumblings, we can be as compassionate with ourselves as we would like to be with others.

Personal Comments

I wonder: how many times have I encountered one of the *Lamed-vav Tzadikim* and never known it? When the letter *Tzadi* comes into my life, I open to the marvelous possibility that someone I just met or will soon encounter could actually be a *Tzadik*. Even that person who really bugs me. Maybe even, in a particular situation, I myself!

For *Tzadikim* are not just out there somewhere, apart from us. Rabbi Cooper writes, "Many of us act as *Lamed-vav Tzadikim* without even knowing it ourselves."[8] The chance word, the kind look, the humorous gesture — who knows what impact our unsuspecting actions might have on someone else? *Tzadi* reminds me: don't take yourself for granted and don't belittle yourself; be a *Tzadik*!

Summary for Tzadi

Numerical value:	90
Meanings:	Righteousness.
Application:	Be alert to the presence of *Tzadikim* in our lives.
	Reweave ourselves into the fabric of community.
	Increase our performance of *mitzvot*, good deeds and *Tzedakah*, charity.
Shadow:	Self-righteousness.
	Berating ourselves for not living up to an unrealistically high standard.
Reflection:	Who in my life have I experienced to be a *Tzadik*? How can I be more *Tzadik*-like myself?
Suggested action:	Perform an anonymous act of *Tzedakah* today.

CHAPTER NINETEEN

KUF

(koof)

SOUND: *k*

NUMERICAL VALUE: 100

Meanings

"*Kadosh, kadosh, kadosh!*" sings Isaiah. "Holy, holy, holy!" *Kuf* is a letter of holiness. It begins the words *kedushah*, "holiness"; *kiddush*, "to make holy"; *kaddish*, "praise of God's holiness"; and קדוש, *kadosh*, "holy."

One of the ancient ways of expressing holiness was through *korban*, "sacrifice." This *Kuf*-initiated word comes from the Hebrew root קרב, *karav*, meaning "to come close" or "draw near." Offerings and sacrifice provide a way to come closer to the Divine.

The body of teachings about how to experience and live a holy life is called קבלה, *Kabbalah*. *Kabbalah* comes from the root קבל, *kabal*, "to receive" and means "receiving."

Kuf equals one hundred, which is a number of completion and perfection, the fulfillment of a cycle. The word "holy" is related to "whole." When a cycle is complete, wholeness/holiness is fulfilled. *Kuf* is central to the words *hakaf*, "to go around," and *hakafa*, "cycle." In Jewish wedding ceremonies, the bride circles the groom seven times. During the holiday of *Simchat Torah*, which celebrates the completion of one annual cycle of Torah readings and the beginning of the next, the Torah scroll itself is processed in a circle around the synagogue. These *hakafot*, circlings, have the power to elicit heightened spiritual states.

The paradox of *Kuf* is that this letter of completion and wholeness is itself broken. *Kuf* is one of only two letters in the *Aleph Beit* (*Hei* is the other one) consisting of two unattached parts. It is also the only letter whose regular form (not final-letter form) descends below the line of writing.

Application

Kuf, as one hundred, marks the end of an old cycle and the beginning of a new one. Endings always involve some sort of death. The leg of *Kuf* descends below the line of writing into the underworld. *Kuf* lives in both worlds. It challenges us to make peace with change, to find the holiness, the wholeness, within loss and new beginnings.

In several places in the Jewish liturgy, worshippers recite *kaddish* prayers, prayers of thanks for the Divine's holiness. This prayer, as the Mourner's Kaddish, is recited daily during the first eleven months of mourning and thereafter on the yearly anniversary of the death. The *kaddish*, rather than bemoaning loss, affirms the goodness of the Holy One. *Kuf*, as the first letter of *kaddish*, calls us to similar affirmation of wholeness in the face of change and impermanence.

Kuf is broken, composed of two separate parts. This suggests that our holiness, our wholeness, exists right in the midst of our brokenness or maybe even because of it. Life is a series of lettings-go. Being able to both grieve the losses and also joyously welcome the new is the challenge of holiness, the challenge of *Kuf*.

Korban, sacrifice, involves giving up something, letting something die, in order to keep the cycle of life flowing. The English word "sacrifice" literally means "make sacred." *Kuf* calls us to make some form of sacrifice, some type of offering in acknowledgment of all that we take in the course of being alive. What are we willing to offer back to the source of life? In the days of the Temple in Jerusalem, burnt animal offerings were given. Nowadays, animals are no longer offered, but something still must be sacrificed. Such offerings can take the form of food or wine or prayers or songs or creations of our hands or even just our tears.

While *korban*, sacrifice, involves letting go, *Kabbalah* involves receiving or welcoming in. *Kuf* signifies a time of receptivity. The letter's very brokenness can be a sign to open our hearts and minds to new inspiration and teachings.

There are two traditional approaches to *Kabbalah*. In one, teachings are received from a teacher in a direct, person-to-person transmission. In the other approach, inspiration and insight flow directly to the student from the Divine. *Kuf* calls us to open to inspiration from human guides and/or direct transmission from the Unknowable.[1]

In the Unknowable, all ideas of holiness disappear. When the Chinese emperor asked Bodhidharma, the famous sage who brought Buddhism from India to China, what was the highest teaching of Buddhism, Bodhidharma answered, "Vast emptiness, nothing holy."

The emperor didn't understand, and he continued, "Who are you then?" In other words, "How can you say there's nothing holy? Aren't you a holy man?"

Bodhidharma responded, "I don't know."

Fundamentally, there is no holiness, just profound, complete not-knowingness. *Kuf* calls us to the fundamental openness and receptivity of "I don't know." With the "beginner's mind" of not knowing, we are open to learning. Without a lot of concepts and judgments and pronouncements about "holiness," we can be natural and spontaneous. We can be like a "holy fool," doing what needs to be done without attachment to how "good" or "not good" we are.

We can be like Rabbi Moshe of Kobryn. When one of his disciples was asked what was most important to his teacher, the student replied, "Whatever he happened to be doing at the moment."[2]

At the exact same time that all is vast emptiness with nothing holy, everything is holy! Rabbi Abraham Heschel said, "Just to be is a blessing. Just to live is holy."[3]

Rebbe Nachman advised, "Seek the sacred within the ordinary. Seek the remarkable within the commonplace."[4]

Kuf calls each of us to express the holiness that is not holiness and to remember: "Just to live is holy."

Kuf's Shadow

Becoming over-attached to an idea of "holiness" is one problematic aspect of *Kuf*. This can set up polarized, dichotomous thinking in which we deny the multifaceted and ambiguous nature of life in favor of some idealized purity. Often, this ideal involves a condemnation of the body or physical side of life. Shame is the flipside of an out-of-balance concern with holiness, shame over having a body or sharing common human foibles and failings. *Kuf* takes us in hand, exhorting us to be holy, but reminding us of the brokenness within wholeness.

Projecting our own insecurities and weaknesses onto others is another common pitfall of this letter. In patriarchal traditions, for example, responsibility for the fall from holiness has been ascribed to women. In this way of thinking, women are weak and sinful and lure men away from holiness. It's all Eve's fault, in other words. The receptivity that *Kuf* demands includes being open to taking responsibility for our own thoughts and actions and not blaming others.

Personal Comments

Did you ever hear the late Rabbi Shlomo Carlebach tell a story? He'd often begin by addressing his audience, "Holy brothers, holy sisters, listen as I tell you the holiest of the holy." The stories that followed were populated by holy beggars, holy husbands, holy wives, holy peddlers, holy *rebbes*, holy street sweepers. Everybody was holy!

Like a Shlomo story, the letter *Kuf* inspires me to look for the holiness in those I meet. Can my personal story be populated by holy bus drivers, holy grocery clerks, holy neighbors, holy colleagues, holy friends? Whether or not such a perspective is possible is really up to me, holy Richard.

ק
Summary for Kuf

Numerical value:	100
Meanings:	Holiness. Completion and fulfillment. Sacrifice.
Application:	Make peace with change and find the holiness, the wholeness, within loss and new beginnings.
	Dedicate a tangible offering to the source of life.
	Be open and alert to receive inspiration and teachings from the human and the Divine.
	Do what needs to be done with a "don't know" mind.
Shadow:	Shame and condemnation of the body.
	Projection of our "unholy" tendencies onto others.
Reflection:	What form of gift am I willing to offer back to the source of life in acknowledgment of all that I have taken in the course of being alive?
Suggested action:	Outdoors, in secret, offer a poem, a picture, a song, wine, food, or prayers, or tears, or some other offering to the Unknowable as a gift. Leave it there and don't tell or show anybody what you have done, and don't go back to visit this spot.

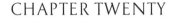

CHAPTER TWENTY

RESH

(rehsh)

SOUND: *r*

NUMERICAL VALUE: 200

Meanings

ריש, *Resh*, shares the same Hebrew root as ראש, *rosh*. *Rosh* means "head" or "beginning" or "new" as in *Rosh Hashanah* (literally "head of the year"). *Resh* powers the words *refuah*, "healing"; *rachamim*, "compassion"; and *rav*, "rabbi" or "teacher."

Resh's Hebrew root, רש, also means "poverty," or a kind of spiritual or moral emptiness, that is independent of how much money one has. In some Kabbalistic teachings, *Resh* is associated with *roah*, "badness," and *rasha*, "to do wrong."

The letter *Resh*, therefore, is itself a *rav*, teaching us about healing and compassion and also doing wrong. Let's see how we can learn *Resh*'s lessons in the most positive, least painful way.

Application

Another name for *Rosh Hashanah* is *Yom Hazikaron*, the Day of Remembrance. *Rosh Hashanah* involves looking back over the previous year and remembering one's actions, for better and worse. The

Hebrew word for sin, *cheit*, literally means "miss the mark." At the beginning of the new year, we recall those times in the previous year when we missed the mark, when we did not live up to our ideals.

Have we indulged in *yetzer hara*, "the evil impulse"; *lashon hara*, "the evil tongue"; and *ayin hara*, "the evil eye"? These habits are insidious. Even when we're earnestly trying to avoid them, before we know it, we've transgressed again. Deliberately indulging in such destructive habits leads to a kind of moral *resh*, moral poverty.

A new beginning is possible, though. The twenty-two letters of the *Aleph Beit* are considered the primordial building blocks of creation. As one of these twenty-two building blocks, *Resh* with its meaning as "new" shows that the power of renewal is built into the very structure of existence. *Ra'ananut*, "freshness," is present at every moment. (*Ra'ananut* begins with *Resh*, and the English word "fresh" even has a "resh" in it.)

While freshness is possible for each of us at every moment, the ten-day period between *Rosh Hashanah* and *Yom Kippur* is especially designated as a time of renewal for all Jews. *Rosh Hashanah* marks a time of introspection and *teshuvah*, "repentance" and "return."

Repentance literally means "rethinking" or "thinking again." As we remember, we repent. *Teshuvah*, repentance, is considered so basic and necessary an underpinning of existence that the Talmud lists it as one of the seven forces that existed even before the creation of the universe. Without repentance, the universe could not exist!

After repentance comes return. Individually and collectively, we return to the intention to live up to our highest ideals in the year to come.

When the letter *Resh* appears in our hands, it may be time for a personal, mini-*Rosh Hashanah*. It is an opportunity to take stock of our actions and return again to the core of who we are. We don't have to wait until the fall appearance of the official holiday to "do *teshuvah*."

"Return again, return again, return to the home of your soul. Return to who you are, return to what you are, return to where you are, born and reborn again," goes a song of *Resh*.[1] To return is to turn again, to come back. Have we lost our way in this confusing world?

Have we lost sight of who we are or who we want to be? Have we lost a sense of connection with the Divine? The letter *Resh* calls to us, "Turn around! Come back! Return again!"

The word *rav* means "archer" as well as "rabbi" or "teacher." If committing a *cheit*, a sin, means to miss the mark, then *Resh* is the *rav*, the archer, who attempts to hit it. *Resh* urges us to aim carefully. When we hit the mark, *refuah*, healing, is the prize.

Another *Rosh Hashanah* tradition is that of *tashlich*, "sending away." At a stream or lake or other body of water, people say prayers and cast crumbs or stones into the water that symbolize habits or actions or memories from the previous year that they want to let go of and send away.

Resh can be an incentive to perform our own version of *tashlich*. We don't have to wait until *Rosh Hashanah* to ceremonially cast away guilt or regrets, and start afresh.

Resh calls us to develop our "inner *rav*," our inner rabbi and teacher. As we do this, we embody more fully the qualities of *Resh* as head and leader. We lead ourselves toward *refuah*, healing and wholeness, when, with *rachamim*, compassion, we strive to hit the mark. With such a spirit, we may find ourselves naturally becoming leaders of others. *Resh* encourages confidence in these leadership qualities.

In writing about the "spiritual traps" that deter people from taking leadership and "cut the nerve of compassionate action," Robert Aitken says, "I would add one more trap: that we do not feel confident of ourselves as movers and shakers. We are conscious of our own limitations and neuroses, and we feel that by speaking out and acting we will only impose our problems on the world. Well, there have been no leaders without limitations and neuroses, not one. We are all human. The problems are out there for us to deal with as we are."[2]

"Lead on!" *Resh* urges.

Resh's Shadow

It is possible to become fixated on evil, projecting evil onto others or identifying ourselves as excessively sinful. *Resh* doesn't shy away from naming evil, but as the first letter of *rachamim*, compassion, it maintains a spirit of compassion even as it identifies what is sinful. If we veer into being judgmental and self-righteous, we have moved into *Resh's* shadow.

Resh calls for compassion for ourselves as well. *Cheit*, sin, means missing the mark, and even the best archer doesn't hit a bullseye with every shot. Most important are the intention and willingness to do *teshuvah* and return to our ideals, not to flagellate ourselves for our failings.

Resh's shadow can lead us to denigrate the body as sinful or view emotions as weak and shameful. *Teshuvah* means returning to wholeness, which includes body and mind and emotion. This return to wholeness is also known as *refuah*, healing.

Leadership is easily abused. *Resh*, as leader, can veer toward egotism, arrogance, and corruption. We must remain vigilant to guard against these sometimes subtle and insidious tendencies.

Personal Comments

The head of *Resh* is bent over to the left. Some commentators say this is a sign of its humility. For me, it feels more like shame. Being Jewish, I am no stranger to shame. As a child, even though my parents were kind and relatively nonjudgmental, I felt guilty for many things. I internalized a *Resh*-like negative judgment of my body and its natural urgings.

As an adult, I feel ashamed of the tremendous damage I inflict on the environment through such modern habits as driving a car, flying in planes, consuming electricity and natural gas, buying things packed in plastic, etc. If sinning is missing the mark, sometimes I feel I am several hundred miles off target in the way I live my life.

Resh doesn't let me off the hook easily. It calls me to look carefully at my life. To become aware of how I condone and endorse our enslavement of what we call "matter" for human convenience without giving back. I can't escape the situation, but at least, with bended neck, I can grieve it.

ר

Summary for Resh

Numerical value:	200
Meanings:	Head. New. Poverty.
Application:	Have a mini *"Rosh Hashanah"* by practicing *teshuvah*, repenting of "missing the mark" and returning to our core values.
	Developing one's "inner rabbi."
Shadow:	Being judgmental and self-righteous.
	Condemning our bodies or emotions as sinful.
	Abusing the power of leadership.
Reflection:	What are some areas of my life in need of *refuah*, healing? How might I move toward greater health and wholeness in these areas?
Suggested action:	Do a form of *tashlich*, symbolically casting away what you want to let go of by casting crumbs into water or writing what you repent of on scraps of paper and then burning them.

CHAPTER TWENTY-ONE

SHIN

(shihn)

SOUND: *s* OR *sh*

NUMERICAL VALUE: 300

Meanings

Shin is the letter of אש, *esh*, "fire." *Sefer Yetzirah*, the *Book of Creation*, identifies *Shin* as one of the three "Mother letters" of the *Aleph Beit*, along with *Aleph*, which represents air, and *Mem*, which stands for water. (*Shin* combines with *Aleph* to form the word *esh*, just as fire combines with air in order to burn.) The ends of *Shin*'s three upraised arms resemble the flames of a fire, and *Shin*'s sound is like the hissing of a flame. The Hebrew word for sun, שמש, *shemesh*, begins and ends with *Shin*. *Shin* also sparks the fire and sun-related words of *sh'viv*, "spark"; *shalhevet*, "flame"; and *sharav*, "heat."

Shin initiates the profound word שלום, *shalom*. *Shalom*, which is one of the names for God, conveys a host of meanings including: peace, wholeness, fullness, completion, soundness, safety, health, intactness, integrity, perfection.

Another name for God, שדי, *Shaddai*, begins with *Shin*. *Shaddai* comes from the Hebrew roots שד, *shad*, "breast," and די, *dai*, "enough." God is that which is enough or has enough. God is the "enoughness" that pervades and feeds the universe. The milk from the breasts of their animals was the very sustenance of life for the sheep-herding and goat-herding nomadic Hebrews. *Shaddai*, as a name for God, therefore represents ancient, primal, life-giving feminine force.

Shaddai, or more often just its first letter, *Shin*, appears on the doorposts of Jewish homes throughout the world, inscribed on the outside of the *mezzuzah*, the small case that contains a piece of parchment with the "*Shema Yisrael*" prayer (Deu. 6:4-9). This central prayer, which Jews are taught to utter as their final words before death, also begins with the powerful Mother letter, *Shin*.

Shin's name and the word *shanah*, year (as in *Rosh Hoshanah*, "head of the year") are both related to the Hebrew root for "change," שנה, *shinah*. A year could be described as one continuous process of change. *Shin* is its symbol.

Punctuating the year every seven days is שבת, *Shabbat*. *Shabbat*, which begins with *Shin*, is the day set aside in the midst of change to experience and celebrate "enoughness." On *Shabbat* we welcome into our lives the שכינה, *Shechinah*, the Sabbath Queen, the feminine aspect of God.

Infusing *Shalom*, *Shaddai*, *Shabbat*, and *Shechinah* with its powerful energy, *Shin* also initiates that happiest of Hebrew words, שמחה, *simcha*, joy.

Application

When *Shin* lights its way into awareness, it's an opportune time to feel graced with the blessings of *shalom*. *Shin* reassures us that right now, at this moment, we are safe, that all is whole and complete and well. *Simcha* is at hand.

"Yeah, right," the cynical or skeptical, or maybe practical, part of us thinks. "The world is full of terrible suffering, and my life is not in such hot shape, either. How can you say all is well?"

Shin is not a letter of facile theories. It contains the primal power of fire. As one of the three "Mothers" of the *Aleph Beit*, *Shin* is one of the building blocks of the building blocks. It burns away superficialities and gets to the core of experience. And at the core of experience, when everything else is burned away by *Shin*'s holy fire, dwells *shalom*.

Even in times of doubt, or sickness, or grief, or war, when all seems dark, *Shin* burns like an ember in an otherwise cold fireplace. Fire lives in that ember, holding the potential that flames can spark back to life, that profound peace can blaze up and warm our hearts once again. If we are experiencing a "dark night of the soul," *Shin* carries the promise that light and warmth are close at hand.

Shin challenges us to feel — at least for a few moments — satisfied, not grasping after anything else, not feeling that if only we had this or that, then we would be happy. We are intact, whole right now, *Shin* teaches, with nothing lacking. We have enough, nourished by *Shaddai*, the Sufficient One.

When *Shin*, the symbol of both change and peace, blazes its way into our lives, we are challenged to find *shalom*, wholeness, intactness, right in the midst of change. Everything is changing constantly, and yet at the center, there is something that does not change. This point of *shalom*, this still point, is the secret of *Shabbat* and the secret of *Shaddai*, being peaceful and feeling that what we have, at least for the time being, is enough. This is the key to *simcha*, joy.

A *shanah*, year, is marked by the changing seasons. Yet the thirteenth-century Zen master Wu-men wrote, "There is a spring that does not belong to *yin* and *yang*."[1] He taught that we can experience a season that is not subject to coming and going, to birth and death, to yearly cycles of change. It is possible to enjoy the spring that does not belong to *yin* and *yang* right now, even as we shiver in the winter rain or seek the shade on a hot summer day.

Inscribed on the *mezzuzah* by the threshold, the locus of coming and going, *Shin* stands as a reminder of the place where there is no coming or going. *Shin* teaches that change and peace share a common origin. As we make peace with change, find peace within change, then we actually experience the power of *Shaddai*. It is enough.

Nanao Sakaki writes:

Just Enough
Soil for legs
Axe for hands
Flowers for eyes
Bird for ears
Mushroom for nose
Smile for mouth
Song for lungs
Sweat for skin
Wind for mind[2]

This is *Shin*'s message: just enough. The world is offering us just enough. Just as we place our foot down, the ground meets it. As the alarm clock rings, we roll over and turn it off. As the baby cries, we pick her up. What else is there, after all, but this, our changing, changeless life?

Shin, as the letter of fire, calls for heat, for passion, for excitement, for fun. *Shin* invites us to cultivate *simcha*, joy. Rebbe Nachman said, "Always remember: joy is not merely incidental to your spiritual quest. It is vital." He also said, "Finding true joy is the hardest of all spiritual tasks. If the only way to make yourself happy is by doing something silly, do it."[3]

Shin, this profound letter of change and *Shabbat* and *shalom* and fire, also kindles silliness and fun. Enjoy! Enjoy!

Shin's Shadow

Fire is powerful, with the potential to get out of control. *Shin*'s flames of passion can turn destructive. Anger, lust, and jealousy can burst into great conflagrations. People can get burned. Instead of providing light and warmth, *Shin* can burn down the house.

As always, balance is called for. The Hebrew word for heaven, שמים, *shamayim*, is composed of the letter of fire, *Shin*, plus the word for water, מים, *mayim*. The water tempers the fire and the fire warms the water. Together, they create holy steam. To experience some of the *simcha* of *shamayim,* we must aspire to that middle place where water and fire coexist, each maintaining its power without raging out of control into damaging floods or destructive infernos.

Personal Comments

There's something ancient and evocative about a campfire at night under the open sky. We stare into the ever-changing flames, hearing their crackle and hiss, feeling their warmth, smelling the rich wood smoke as it rises up. Enhanced by the fire's magic, stories and songs and laughter naturally come forth. It becomes easy to imagine our ancestors, sharing their own stories and songs and laughter around similar fires, for hundreds and thousands of years.

There's something ancient and evocative about the letter *Shin,* also. It, too, sparks *ma'asiya,* "story"; and *shir,* "song"; and *s'hok,* "laughter." Like fire, it, too, is primordial and powerful. As I gaze at its shape on the page, imagining it as black fire on white fire, *Shin* fills me with a sense of awesome mystery. In the world of change, *Shin* reminds me of the power of *Shaddai,* Enough, the power of things as they are.

Summary for Shin

Numerical value:	300
Meanings:	Fire. *Shalom*, peace, wholeness. *Shaddai*, enoughness. Change. *Simcha*, joy.
Application:	Experience *shalom* even in the midst of change.
	Practice feeling satisfied, filled with "enough."
	Cultivate joy.
Shadow:	Consuming or being consumed by flames of anger, lust, jealousy, etc.
Reflection:	How might I increase the amount of joy I experience in my life?
Suggested action:	Practice *simcha* by maintaining a half-smile on your face at various times during the day. Observe how this half-smile makes you feel and how it affects your interactions with others.

CHAPTER TWENTY-TWO

TAV

(tahv)

SOUND: *t*

NUMERICAL VALUE: 400

Meanings

Tav, as the final letter of the *Aleph Beit*, signifies endings and consummation. Like the English phrase "from A to Z," the saying "from *Aleph* to *Tav*" expresses completeness. The word תו, *Tav*, means a mark, seal, impression, or stamp. *Tav* seals the Hebrew alphabet, leaving its mark of fulfillment.

There is no ending without a new beginning, however. According to Rabbi Michael Munk, "Kabbalistic literature teaches that the *Aleph Beit* — representing all divine forces — does not culminate with the *Tav* but turns around to unite again with the *Aleph*."[1]

Similarly, *Sefer Yetzirah*, the Book of Creation, says, "Their end is embedded in their beginning and their beginning in their end."[2] Even as it represents termination, *Tav* suggests there is more to come. In fact, in Aramaic, the ancient cousin language to Hebrew, the word *Tav* means "more," "again," "further." Beyond what appears to be an end, there is always something more. The left foot of *Tav* protrudes out, moving forward (since Hebrew reads from right to left) into the future.

Tav initiates *tamid*, the word for "always" or "forever." The *Aleph Beit* begins with *Aleph* and ends with *Tav*, but the creative vibrations of the letters continue on forever, always fresh and new.

Some of the words in which *Aleph* and *Tav* unite are especially profound and important. For example, אמת, *emet*, "truth," is created when *Aleph*, the first letter of the *Aleph Beit*, unites with *Mem*, a middle letter, and *Tav*, the last. Truth, the essential fact of things, pervades the universe, "from *Aleph* to *Tav*."

Many of the basic forms of Jewish observance begin with *Tav* such as *tefillah*, "prayer"; *tehillim*, "psalms"; and *teshuvah*, "returning" or "repentance." The last letter of the *Aleph Beit* is the first letter of the names of the basic texts of Judaism, תורה, *Torah*; תלמוד, *Talmud*; and תנייך, *Tanach*, the twenty-four books of the Old Testament.

Tav initiates one of the most crucial terms in Kabbalistic practice, תקון, *tikkun*. *Tikkun* means "to repair" or "to redeem." Rabbi Isaac Luria taught that the ultimate task of each person is to contribute to the mending of a shattered universe, unifying sparks of holiness through perceiving the inherent sacredness of all things. If this is our ultimate task, how appropriate then that the *Aleph Beit* culminates with this sign of *tikkun*, the letter *Tav*.

Application

When *Tav*, the "mark," leaves its mark on us, a cycle has come to an end. *Tav* puts the seal on a process of completion. It's over.

Such times can be bittersweet, like graduations or retirements. Or terribly sad, like divorces or deaths. Or fulfilling, like the completion of a large and satisfying project. They can be joyful, as the end of one cycle marks the beginning of a new one, as in weddings and births. But, one way or another, for better or worse, *Tav* signifies culmination.

As the letter of *emet*, truth, *Tav* calls us to confront the truth of the situation, to face the facts. *Tav* marks a natural time for reflection on the process that has just ended. Some of the questions this letter raises are:

- "What have I learned from this experience?"
- "What blessings did I receive?"
- "What blessings did I give?"
- "Where do I go from here?"

We have seen that *Tav* initiates *tefillah*, prayer. Prayers often arise during periods of ending, transition, and reflection — prayers of grief, prayers of gratitude, prayers for guidance and direction. *Tav* may signify a time of *teshuvah*, returning or repentance, as we return to an awareness of the sacred or to ourselves, or repent for mistakes made.

Endings and new beginnings provide excellent opportunities to commit ourselves anew to *tikkun*, repair or rectification. Ever since Rabbi Isaac Luria emphasized the concept more than four hundred years ago, *tikkun* has assumed a vital importance in Jewish mystical practice. Rabbi Luria taught that we uplift and redeem the fallen sparks of holiness that are hidden in "husks" within every thing, by means of our prayers, our deepened awareness, and our acts of loving-kindness.

I believe that for those of us living in the decades after the holocaust of World War II, our impulse for *tikkun* is an attempt to somehow redeem the millions of souls who perished in the concentration camps and were murdered in the trenches.

Tav urges us to strive for *tikkun* in our own lives and in our own ways. How might we do that? Contemporary Rabbi David Cooper writes, "Our opportunities to raise sparks are boundless. The choices we make for our activities, the interactions we have with our family, friends, neighbors, business associates, and even strangers, the way we spend our leisure time, the books we read, the television we watch, the way we relate to food, everything in daily life presents sparks locked in husks awaiting release."[3]

As we release these sparks, we actually help prepare the way for the complete redemption of the world through the manifestation of *Mashiach* consciousness. "The appearance of the Messiah is nothing but the consummation of the continuous process of restoration, of *tikkun*," writes scholar Gershom Scholem. "The *tikkun*, the path to the end of all things, is also the path to the beginning."[4]

Tav, this letter of ending and beginning, of *tikkun* and Torah, of prayers and *teshuvah*, makes a big impression, indeed. It calls us to leave our own marks in the world, through our prayers, our awareness, and our acts of loving-kindness.

Tav's Shadow

Sometimes we end a situation or relationship prematurely in order to avoid the risks of deeper intimacy or involvement. Has the situation had a chance to reach its resolution, its natural culmination, or are we forcing a too-early end out of our own fears or doubts? It can be hard to know at times. (On the other hand, sometimes, because of fears or doubts, we remain in situations or relationships beyond a healthy end point, refusing to let go.)

Tav marks a resolution, a completion, a consummation. This can take many forms beyond an obvious "ending." We must be careful not to interpret *Tav* too literally or simplistically. After all, it's as much a letter of new beginnings as it is a letter of endings.

A danger in the concept of *tikkun* is the assumption that the world is inherently flawed, and that it's up to us somehow to rectify the problem. This is especially pernicious when we apply it literally to another person. While opportunities for "repair" are obvious all around us, in another sense, the world is complete just as it is. Excessive focus on the shattered nature of things can drag us down and burn us out. Waiting for the Messiah to appear can cause us to disparage this present life. *Tav*'s challenging task is to engage in *tikkun* with joy, even as tears of sorrow flow as we confront the brokenness of the world.

Personal Comments

Even as it ends the *Aleph Beit*, *Tav* keeps moving on down the line, its left foot stepping out into the future. *Tav* reminds me of a song by the famous blues musicians Sonny Terry and Brownie McGhee: "Walk on, walk on, walk on, walk on. I'm gonna keep on walkin' til I find my way back home." Sturdy, intrepid *Tav* walks on. Just as we do when one situation ends, and we move forward into the next incarnation of our lives.

ת
Summary for Tav

Numerical value:	400
Meanings:	Mark, seal, impression. Torah. *Tefillah*, prayer. Talmud. *Tikkun*, repair and redemption.
Application:	Acknowledge and reflect on the completion of a process or cycle. Offer prayers of grief or gratitude, or for guidance. Commit oneself to striving for *tikkun*.
Shadow:	Ending situations or relationships prematurely. Conversely, clinging to situations or relationships beyond a healthy end point. Focusing excessively on the "broken" aspects of life.
Reflection:	What have I learned from a significant experience which recently came to a close? What blessings did I receive? What blessings did I give? Where do I go from here?
Suggested action:	Complete a tangible act of *tikkun* today. What can you uplift, repair, put right, or redeem?

CHAPTER TWENTY-THREE

The Missing Letter

SOUND: ?

NUMERICAL VALUE: ?

Meanings

The twenty-second letter, *Tav*, completes the *Aleph Beit*. Or does it? A thirteenth-century Kabbalistic text, *Sefer Ha-Temunah* (*The Book of the Image*), teaches that one letter is missing from the current *Aleph Beit*. Every defect in our present world stems from the absence of this letter. When, at some point in the future, this letter is revealed, then all the defects will disappear. This missing consonant, whose sound is unimaginable, inconceivable, will then combine with all the other letters to create new words, new worlds. Finally, all will be complete.

A Talmudic legend tells that this twenty-third letter appeared on the original set of tablets upon which the Ten Utterances were inscribed. When the tablets were broken because the Israelites worshipped the golden calf, all the letters flew off the tablets and ascended to Heaven. The other twenty-two letters eventually returned, but the twenty-third letter had vanished from this world.[1]

Some Jewish mystics speculate that the form of this letter is similar to a *Shin* with four heads instead of three. On the right side of the *tefillin*, the small, black leather box worn on the head during morning prayers, is embossed a regular, three-headed *Shin*. But on the left side, commemorating the missing letter, is embossed a mysterious four-headed *Shin*.

The Zohar describes *Shin* as "the letter of the fathers." The three prongs on the *Shin* on the *tefillin*'s right side represent the three fathers, Abraham, Isaac, and Jacob.[2] The four prongs on the *Shin* on the *tefillin*'s left side symbolize the four mothers, Sarah, Rebecca, Rachel, and Leah.[3]

In the future, when the missing letter, the letter of the left side, is revealed, the world will be balanced once again. Then, the letter of the mothers, lost for so long, will combine with all the other letters to create a universe of harmony and peace.

Application

The twenty-third letter is a sign of promise, of yet unrealized potential. Even though the four-headed *Shin* on the left side of the *tefillin* hints at it, we really don't know what this letter will look like, let alone what it will sound like. It represents the undreamed of, the unimaginable, the possible.

What might life be like in a universe where harmony and wholeness actually thrived? Where "the letter of the mothers" had as much presence and substance as "the letter of the fathers"? Where every defect had disappeared?

Some say that the missing letter will appear only when the Messiah appears. The revelation of the twenty-third letter will usher in the Messianic age, or conversely, the appearance of the Messiah will create the conditions for the missing letter to come into awareness once again.

The word for "messiah" in Hebrew, משיח, *Mashiach*, begins with *Mem*, the letter of the feminine powers of womb and water, and continues with *Shin*, the letter of the masculine power of fire. Similarly, the word for wholeness, harmony, completeness, שלום, *shalom*, combines the energy of *Shin* and *Mem*.

Like the *tefillin*, with the letter of the fathers on the right side and the letter of the mothers on the left, the Messianic age will be marked by the harmonious blending of the masculine and the feminine. Then, the *Shechinah*, the feminine, immanent aspect of the Divine, will be united with the masculine, transcendent aspect, and a new Eden will flourish.

But what do we do in the meantime, just wait? Well, patience is indeed important. Choosing this letter can be a reminder to view things from a truly long-range perspective, beyond that of human lifetimes.

At the same time, however, we need not be passive. We can make the best of the present even while praying and yearning and working for a better future. Rabbi Hillel asked, "If not now, when?" Can we experience wholeness and harmony in the present? The road to the future travels through this very moment. Can we embody some of the qualities of the Messianic age right now?

One of them, for example, is humor. "In the deepest depths, humor is a little bit of the taste of the coming of the Messiah. Because when the Messiah comes, our mouths will be filled with laughter," writes Susan Yael Mesinai.[4]

Part of this humor is the cosmic laughter that comes when we realize we have no idea what's going on! Even as we're filled with yearning for the ideal, perfect future, part of us sees the absurdity of our plight. Our ignorance of what the twenty-third letter looks like or sounds like is just like our fundamental ignorance about everything.

The tenth-century Zen teacher Ti-tsang asked the wandering monk Fa-yen where he was going. Fa-yen answered that he was on pilgrimage, going wherever his feet will carry him.

Ti-tsang said, "What do you expect from pilgrimage?"

Fa-yen said, "I don't know."

Ti-tsang then replied, "Ah, not-knowing is most intimate."[5]

Each of us is intimate with not-knowing. It's the very heart of our experience. Part of the message of the missing letter is to make peace with not-knowing, to accept with good humor this basic ignorance.

> "I see nobody on the road," said Alice. "I only wish I had such eyes," the King remarked in a fretful tone. "To be able to see Nobody, and at such a distance, too!"[6]

When we choose this letter, we may feel like Alice in Wonderland. There's nobody to see on this card's face. The twenty-third letter is the letter of dreams, of fairy tales, of an alternate reality. It calls us to walk forward into the next crazy adventure of life, not knowing what will come next or what strange characters we will encounter.

This missing letter also signifies that sound beyond all sounds. It represents the last word, the word beyond all words. When choosing this letter, perhaps the best response is just to keep quiet. Words and letters will never truly describe the essence of life.

Rumi said,

> I have no more words.
> Let the soul speak
> with the silent articulation
> of a face.[7]

Shadow

One shadow aspect of the twenty-third letter is abandoning the present because a better world supposedly waits in the future. The apocalyptic fantasies and even longing for world destruction on the part of many fundamentalist groups represent an extreme version of this future-oriented view that disparages this world, this earth, this moment.

The attitude that a better world waits in the future may be expressed through apathy or despair about the present, giving up on life, or acting self-destructively. The missing letter promises a better future, but that doesn't mean we should malign the present. It's all we have.

Personal Comments

When I ponder this missing letter I feel a deep, aching longing. I yearn and I yearn, and I'm not sure what exactly I'm yearning for. The dream of wholeness, maybe, the hope of peace, of joy? A place where people and animals and birds and fish and all the beings of the earth are able to live in balance and fulfillment according to their natures?

The twenty-third letter is the emblem of our deepest desires. Its mysterious, unknown shape and form receives and holds our hopes and dreams and aspirations. The missing letter carries the promise that somehow, someday, *shalom*, wholeness, will fill the universe.

Summary for the Missing Letter

There is no summary for the missing letter. How can one summarize a mystery? The missing letter is the letter of the future, the letter of the unknown, the letter of all sounds, the letter of silence.

NOTES

Preface

1. Abraham Abulafia, quoted in Gershom Scholem, *Major Trends in Jewish Mysticism* (New York: Schocken Books, 1974), p. 134.

Introduction

1. Marcia Prager, *The Path of Blessing* (New York: Bell Tower, 1998), p. 191.

2. David Abram, *The Spell of the Sensuous* (New York: Vintage Books, 1997), p. 245.

3. Harry Sperling and Maurice Simon, trans., *The Zohar,* vol. 2 (London: Soncino Press, 1978), p. 111.

4. Daniel Matt, trans., *The Zohar: The Book of Enlightenment* (New York: Paulist Press, 1983), p. 120.

5. Jiri Langer, *Nine Gates to the Hasidic Mysteries* (New York: David McKay Company, 1961), p. 16.

6. Baal Shem Tov, quoted in Prager, *The Path of Blessing,* p. 192.

7. Abram, *The Spell of the Sensuous*, p. 242.

8. Ibid, p. 243.

9. Stephen Mitchell, trans., *Genesis* (New York: HarperCollins, 1996), p. xiv.

10. Deuteronomy 18:10-13.

11. See Exodus 28:15-30.

12. *Encyclopaedia Judaica*, Vol. 6 (Jerusalem: Keter Publishing, 1996), p. 117.

13. Abraham Abulafia, *Life of the Future World*, 1280, quoted in John Matthews, ed., *The World Atlas of Divination* (Boston, Toronto & New York: Little, Brown and Company, 1992), p. 74.

14. Quoted in Edward Hoffman, *The Heavenly Ladder* (East Meadow, NY: Four Worlds Press, 1985), p. 120.

15. Isaiah 7:11.

16. For suggestions regarding consulting oracles see Dianne Skafte, *Listening to the Oracle* (HarperSanFrancisco, 1997), p. 32.17.

17. Perle Epstein, *Kaballah: The Way of the Jewish Mystic* (Boston: Shambhala, 1988), pp. 98-99.

18. Abraham Abulafia, quoted in Hoffman, *The Heavenly Ladder,* p. 125.

19. Abraham Joshua Heschel, *The Quest for God* (New York: Charles Scribner's Sons, 1954), p. xii.

Chapter 1: Aleph

1. In modern Hebrew, when a vowel symbol is placed below Aleph, one pronounces that vowel sound.

2. Aryeh Kaplan, *Meditation and Kabbalah* (York Beach, Maine: Samuel Weiser, 1982), p. 299.

3. Genesis 1:2.

4. Martin Buber, *Tales of the Hasidim: Early Masters* (New York: Schocken Books, 1947), p. 199.

5. Rabbi Yerachmiel Ben Yisrael, quoted in Rami M. Shapiro, ed. and trans., *Open Secrets: The Letters of Reb Yerachmiel Ben Yisrael* (North Carolina: Human Kindness Foundation, 1994), p. 5.

6. Ibid, p. 28.

7. Proverbs 14:4.

8. Y-H-V-H refers to יהוה Yud-Hei-Vav-Hei. This is the unpronounceable Name of God often translated as "Adonai " or "Lord."

9. Genesis 1:6.

10. Zohar 3:75a.

11. Genesis 28:12-15.

12. Genesis 28:16-17.

Chapter 2: Beit

1. Isaiah 56:7.

2. Robert Aitken, *The Practice of Perfection* (New York and San Francisco: Pantheon, 1994), p. 64.

3. Hakuin Zenji, *Chant in Praise of Zazen,* quoted in Robert Aitken, *Taking the Path of Zen* (San Francisco: North Point Press, 1982), p. 113.

4. Naomi Shihab Nye, *Words Under the Words: Selected Poems* (Portland, Oregon: Eighth Mountain Press, 1994), p. 42.

Chapter 3: Gimmel

1. Robert Bly, *Loving a Woman in Two Worlds* (Garden City, NY: Dial Books, 1985).

2. Pirkei Avot 1:2.

3. Rabbi Shlomo Carlebach, quoted in Peninnah Schram, ed., *Chosen Tales: Stories Told by Jewish Storytellers* (Northvale, NJ: Jason Aronson, 1995), pp. 70-75.

Chapter 4: Dalet

1. Martin Prechtel, *Secrets of the Talking Jaguar* (New York: Tarcher/Putnam, 1998), p. 276.

2. Arthur Green and Barry Holtz, eds. and trans., *Your Word is Fire* (Woodstock, VT: Jewish Lights, 1993), p. 51.

3. Martin Buber, *Tales of the Hasidim, Early Masters* (New York: Schocken Books, 1947), p. 64.

4. Rebbe Nachman of Breslav, quoted in Moshe Mykoff, ed., *The Empty Chair* (Woodstock, VT: Jewish Lights, 1994), p. 41, 104.

Chapter 5: Hei

1. Nachman of Breslov, quoted in Mykoff, ed., *The Empty Chair*, p.14.

2. Simone Weil, *Waiting for God* (New York: G. P. Putnam's Sons, 1951), p. 105.

3. Exodus 3:2-4.

4. I Kings 19:11-12.

Chapter 6: Vav

1. Scholem, *Major Trends in Jewish Mysticism*, p. 275.

Chapter 7: Zayin

1. Exodus 20:8.

2. Genesis Rabba 10:9.

3. Abraham Joshua Heschel, *The Sabbath* (New York: Farrar, Straus and Giroux, 1979), p. 19.

4. Deuteronomy Rabba, 3,1.

5. Robert Bly, *Iron John* (New York: Addison-Wesley Publishing Company, 1990), p. 4.

Chapter 8: Chet

1. Job 26:7.
2. Martin Buber, *Tales of the Hasidim, Later Masters* (New York: Schocken Books, 1948), p. 92.
3. Wu-men, quoted in Aitken, *Taking the Path of Zen*, p. 96.
4. Gary Snyder, *Turtle Island* (New York: New Directions, 1974), p. 68.
5. Aryeh Kaplan, *Inner Space* (Brooklyn, NY: Moznaim Publishing Co., 1990), p.167.

Chapter 9: Tet

1. Genesis 1:4.
2. Exodus 4:2-4.
3. Numbers 21:6-9.
4. Buber, *Tales of the Hasidim, Early Masters*, p. 237-238.
5. Psalms 23:4.
6. Psalms 23:6
7. Francesco Patricolo, *"Come the Evolution" on Bop-A-Ganda* (Portland, OR: Willow Sap, 1997).

Chapter 10: Yud

1. Edward Hoffman, *The Hebrew Alphabet: A Mystical Journey* (San Francisco: Chronicle Books, 1998), p. 47.
2. Numbers 12:3.
3. Deuteronomy 7:7.
4. Eruvin 13b; Zohar II 232.
5. Micah 6:8.
6. Jelaluddin Rumi, *The Essential Rumi*, trans. Coleman Barks (HarperSanFrancisco, 1995), p. 279.

Chapter 11: Kaf

1. William Stafford, *Stories that Could Be True* (New York City: Harper and Row, 1977), p. 4.

Chapter 12: Lamed

1. Buber, *Tales of the Hasidim, Early Masters*, p. 313.

2. Rumi, *Illuminated Rumi*, p. 81.

3. Dan Millman, *The Way of the Peaceful Warrior* (Tiburon, CA: H. J. Kramer Inc., 1980), p. 133.

4. Frederick Buechner, *Wishful Thinking: A Theological ABC* (New York. Harper & Row, 1973), p. 95.

Chapter 13: Mem

1. Exodus 34:6-7.

2. Isaiah 11:9.

3. Martin Prechtel, "Grief and Praise: an Evening with Martin Prechtel" (Minneapolis, MN: Hidden Wine Productions, 1997)

4. Rebbe Nachman of Breslav, quoted in Mykoff, ed., *The Empty Chair*, p. 89.

5. Michael Meade, *Men and the Water of Life* (HarperSanFrancisco, 1993), p. 344.

6. Aryeh Hirschfield, *Wings of Peace* (1990).

Chapter 14: Nun

1. Genesis 1:22.

2. Robert Louis Stevenson, *Fables* (New York, 1896).

Chapter 15: Samech

1. Psalms 91:4.

2. Song of Songs 3:8.

3. Martin Luther King, "Letter from a Birmingham Jail."

4. Nakagawa Roshi, quoted in Aitken, *Taking the Path of Zen*, p. 74.

5. Johann Wolfgang von Goethe, "The Holy Longing," trans. Robert Bly, in Bly, Hillman, and Meade, eds., *The Rag and Bone Shop of the Heart* (New York: HarperCollins, 1992), p. 382.

6. Walt Whitman, "Song of Myself" (1855).

Chapter 16: Ayin

1. *Ayin* is a silent letter, but in modern Hebrew when a vowel symbol is placed by *ayin*, one pronounces that vowel sound.

2. Proverbs 29:18.

3. Numbers 11:24-25.

4. Matsuo Bashō in Robert Aitken, *A Zen Wave* (New York: Weatherhill, 1978), p. 74.

5. Rebbe Nachman, quoted in Mykoff, ed., *The Empty Chair*, p. 58.

6. Aitken, *Taking the Path of Zen*, p. 95-96.

7. Meister Eckhart, quoted in Stephen Mitchell, ed., *The Enlightened Mind* (New York: HarperPerennial, 1991), p. 114.

8. Isaiah 52:8.

9. Psalms 119:18.

10. Joel 2:28.

11. Proverbs 27:20.

Chapter 17: Peh

1. Numbers 12:8.

2. Exodus 4:10-16.

3. Proverbs 16:23.

4. Proverbs 15:23.

5. Walpola Rahula, *What the Buddha Taught* (New York: Grove Press, 1959), p. 47.

6. Buber, *Tales of the Hasidim, Later Masters*, p. 229.

7. Matthew 15:11.

8. Robert Aitken, *Encouraging Words* (New York and San Francisco: Pantheon Books, 1993), p. 125.

9. Psalms 51:17

10. Beitzah16a; Rashi.

11. Hil. Teshuvah 2:4.

12. Psalms 19:14.

13. Ecclesiastes 5:3.

Chapter 18: Tzadi

1. Proverbs 10:25.

2. David Cooper, *God is a Verb* (New York: Riverhead Books, 1997), p. 123, 125.

3. Arthur Waskow, *Godwrestling — Round 2* (Woodstock, VT: Jewish Lights, 1996), p. 212.

4. Cooper, *God is a Verb*, p. 242.

5. Ibid, p. 125.

6. Baba Bathra 10b.

7. Aitken, *The Practice of Perfection*, p. 10.

8. Cooper, *God is a Verb*, p. 125.

Chapter 19: Kuf

1. See Cooper, *God is a Verb*, p. 11-12, for a concise description of the two traditional schools of Kabbalah.

2. Buber, *Tales of the Hasidim, Later Masters*, p. 173.

3. Rabbi Abraham Heschel, quoted in Elias Amidon and Elizabeth Roberts, eds., *Earth Prayers* (HarperSanFrancisco, 1991), p. 365.

4. Rebbe Nachman, quoted in Mykoff, ed., *The Empty Chair*, p. 59.

Chapter 20: Resh

1. Raphael Kahn "Return Again," Music by Shlomo Carlebach.

2. Robert Aitken, *The Diamond Sangha Newsletter* (Honolulu, Hawaii: Koko An Zendo, November 1989), p.1.

Chapter 21: Shin

1. Robert Aitken, *The Gateless Barrier* (San Francisco: North Point Press, 1991), p. 142.

2. Nanao Sakaki, *Break the Mirror* (San Francisco: North Point Press, 1987), p. 89.3.

3. Rebbe Nachman, quoted in Mykoff, ed., *The Empty Chair*, p. 99, 101.

Chapter 22: Tav

1. Michael Munk, *The Wisdom in the Hebrew Alphabet* (Brooklyn, NY: Mesorah Publications, 1997), p. 222.

2. Sefer Yetzirah. 1:7.

3. Cooper, *God is a Verb*, p. 29.

4. Scholem, *Major Trends in Jewish Mysticism*, p. 274.

Chapter 23: The Missing Letter

1. Levush HaTecheles 32:43; Pesachim 87b.

2. Zohar 1:2b.

3. Levush, Orach Chaim 32:43.

4. Shlomo Carlebach and Susan Yael Mesinai, *Shlomo's Stories* (Northvale, NJ: Jason Aronson, 1994).

5. Thomas Cleary, trans., *Book of Serenity* (Hudson, NY: Lindisfarne Press, 1990), p. 86.

6. Carroll, *Alice's Adventures*, p. 239.

7. Jalal al-Din Rumi, *Illuminated Rumi*, p. 128.

GLOSSARY

Abulafia, Abraham (1240-1296): Spanish Kabbalist who developed methods of meditating on and combining the letters of the Divine Name in order to reach ecstatic states.

Adonai: A name of God, usually translated in English as "Lord," that is used as a substitute for the unpronounceable four-letter Name יהוה (YHVH). Spelled יי and אדני.

Aleph Beit: The Hebrew alphabet, from the names of the first two letters. Alternatively spelled/pronounced as "*Alef*," "*Beth*," "*Bayt*," "*Bet*," and "*Beis*."

Amidah: The prayer consisting of nineteen blessings that is the core of all Jewish prayer services and that one recites while standing.

Aramaic: Ancient Semitic language closely related to Hebrew.

Aseret ha'Dibrot: Literally, "the Ten Sayings" or "the Ten Utterances." Hebrew phrase used in Torah to describe what are commonly called the "Ten Commandments."

Baal Shem Tov: Literally "Master of the Good Name." The title of Rabbi Israel ben Eliezer (1698-1760), the founder of Hasidism.

Bracha: Blessing.

Chesed: Loving-kindness, grace. One of the ten *Sefirot*.

Chupah: Canopy under which the Jewish wedding ceremony takes place.

Chutzpah: Yiddish for nerve, gumption, audacity.

Ein sof: Literally, "without end" or "without bound." The ultimate, unknowable aspect of God.

Gematria: A system of Jewish mysticism used to gain insight into hidden meanings of the Torah in which one calculates the numerical value of letters, words, and phrases, and then links those letters, words, and phrases with others of the same value.

G'milut chasadim: Acts of loving-kindness.

Golem: Literally, "shapeless mass." A legendary creature made of clay and animated by magical incantations through the letters of the Divine Name.

Ha-shem: Literally, "the Name." Respectful euphemism used as a substitute for naming God.

Hasidism: Mystical movement founded in Poland and the Ukraine in the eighteenth century by the Baal Shem Tov.

Havdalah: Literally, "to distinguish" or "to separate." The ceremony at dusk on Saturday night that marks a separation between *Shabbat* and the new week just beginning.

Kabbalah: Literally, "receiving." The Jewish mystical tradition.

Kavanah: Intention. Meditation or concentration prior to prayer or performance of a holy act.

Koan (Japanese)**:** Literally, "case" (as a court case). An expression of harmony of the relative and the absolute. A theme of meditation to be made clear.

Lamed-Vav Tzadikim or **Lamed-Vavniks:** The thirty-six hidden righteous ones who sustain the world through their merit.

Lashon hara: Literally, "the evil tongue." Gossip, criticism, and other kinds of harmful speech.

Luria, Isaac (1534-1572)**:** Influential Kabbalistic rabbi of Safed, Israel, also known as "the *Ari*," the Lion.

Maggid: A preacher, teacher, healer and storyteller who sometimes travelled a circuit.

Mashiach: The Messiah.

Matzah: Unleavened bread eaten during Passover.

Mezzuzah: Small case containing a piece of parchment with the *Shema* prayer that is attached to the doorposts of houses of Jews.

Midrash: Commentary or extension of Torah, part of the Talmud. Post-Talmudic Jewish legends in general.

Mikveh: A natural body of water or a specially constructed bath used for ceremonies of purification.

Minyan: Quorum of ten adults required for certain ceremonies or prayers. Many congregations require ten men to form a *minyan*, whereas other Jewish groups count both men and women as part of the *minyan*.

Niggunim: Wordless divine melodies.

Omer: The counting of the fifty days from the second night of Passover until *Shavuot*.

Ot: "Letter," "sign," or "miracle."

Reb or Rev: An honorific term used to address a person who is a scholar or a fellow student or disciple.

Rebbe: Yiddish form of "rabbi" used affectionately to refer to Hasidic masters.

Rosh Chodesh: New moon. The beginning of the Hebrew month, marked by special prayers and celebration.

Rosh Hashanah: Literally, "Head of the Year." The Jewish New Year.

Seder: Ritual Passover meal.

Sefer: Book.

Sefer Yetzirah: "The Book of Creation." Earliest known Kabbalistic text, attributed to Rabbi Akiva (2nd century C.E.), which describes how God created the universe by means of the twenty-two Hebrew letters and the ten *Sefirot*.

Sefirot: The ten divine emanations or energies through which the world came into being. Ten branches or containers on the Tree of Life, representing aspects and attributes of the Divine.

Shabbos/Shabbat: Sabbath. The period from sunset Friday night to dusk Saturday night, set aside as a time of rest, renewal, spirituality, and celebration.

Shavuot: The festival that takes place seven weeks after Passover and celebrates the transmission of Torah on Mt. Sinai.

Shechinah: The immanent (as opposed to transcendent), feminine aspect of Divinity. Also referred to as the Sabbath Queen.

Shema: The central prayer of Judaism, from Deuteronomy 6:4-9, "Hear O Israel, YHVH is our God, YHVH is One."

Shmitah: The seventh, sabbatical year, during which the land is not worked.

Shofar: The ram's horn that is ritually blown at *Rosh Hashanah* and *Yom Kippur.*

Simchat Torah: The last day of the harvest festival of *Sukkot,* during which the yearly cycle of reading from the Torah is concluded and then begun again.

Sufi: Mystical branch of Islam, emphasizing ecstatic communion with the Divine through dancing and meditation.

Sukkot: The harvest festival beginning on the full moon after *Rosh Hashanah.*

Sutra (Sanskrit): A discourse or sermon, usually attributed to the Buddha. Buddhist scriptures in general.

Talmud: The collection of rabbinic stories, laws, and teachings written and compiled between 200 B.C.E. and 500 C.E. There are two Talmuds: the Jerusalem Talmud and the Babylonian Talmud. The Talmud interprets Torah and encodes in greater detail the laws that the Torah is supposed to embody. After the Torah, the Talmud is the most sacred Jewish text.

Tanach: The Bible. An acronym combining the initials of *Torah* (the five books of Moses), *Neviim* (Prophets), and *Ketuvim* (Writings).

Tefillin: Phylacteries consisting of two black leather boxes containing Bible verses that are worn on the left arm and the forehead during morning prayers.

Teshuvah: Literally, "return." Repentance or returning.

Tikkun: Literally, "repair." Restoration and redemption, especially, as taught by Isaac Luria, through the raising of sparks of the Divine.

Tikkun olam: Repair of the world.

Torah: The first five books of the Bible. By extension, the whole of Jewish tradition and teaching.

Tzadik: A righteous person, someone known for deep faith and goodness. Hasidim consider their *rebbes* to be *Tzadikim*, possessing great spiritual powers.

Urim and Thummim: The oracular "breastplate of judgment" worn by the High Priest in the Temple.

Yetzer hara: The evil impulse or inclination. Evil spirit.

YHVH: יהוה, *Yud-Hei-Vav-Hei*, the ineffable and unpronounceable, most holy four-letter Name of God, sometimes referred to as "the Tetragrammaton."

Yom Kippur: The Day of Judgment, or the Day of Atonement. The holiest day of the Jewish year, ten days after *Rosh Hashanah*, during which the Holy inscribes peoples' names in the Book of Life for the coming year, thus determining their fates.

Zohar: "The Book of Splendor." Seminal Kabbalistic text compiled from mystical oral traditions by Moshe de Leon in Spain in the thirteenth century.

BIBLIOGRAPHY

On the Hebrew Alphabet

Abram, David. *The Spell of the Sensuous.* New York: Vintage Books, 1997.

Berg, Phillip S. *Power of Aleph Beth, Vol 1.* New York/Jerusalem: Research Center of Kabbalah, 1988.

Drucker, Johanna. *The Alphabetic Labyrinth.* London: Thames and Hudson, 1995.

Ginsburgh, Yitzchak. *The Alef-Beit: Jewish Thought Revealed through the Hebrew Letters.* Northvale, NJ: Jason Aronson, 1995.

Glazerson, Matityahu. *Building Blocks of the Soul: Studies on the Letters and Words of the Hebrew Language.* Northvale, NJ: Jason Aronson, 1997.

——————· *Letters of Fire: Mystical Insights into the Hebrew Language.* Jerusalem & New York: Feldheim Publishers, 1991.

Haralick, Robert M. *The Inner Meaning of the Hebrew Letters.* Northvale, NJ: Jason Aronson, 1995.

Hoffman, Edward. *The Heavenly Ladder: Kabbalistic Techniques for Inner Growth.* East Meadow, NY: Four Worlds Press, 1985.

Hoffman, Edward. *The Hebrew Alphabet: A Mystical Journey.* San Francisco: Chronicle Books, 1998.

Kaplan, Aryeh. *Sefer Yetzirah: The Book of Creation.* York Beach, ME: Samuel Weiser, 1993.

Kushner, Lawrence. *The Book of Letters: A Mystical Alef-bait.* Woodstock, VT: Jewish Lights, 1990.

Munk, Michael. *The Wisdom in the Hebrew Alphabet: The Sacred Letters as a Guide to Jewish Deed and Thought.* Brooklyn, NY: Mesorah Publications, 1997.

Pennick, Nigel. *The Secret Lore of Runes and Other Ancient Alphabets.* London: Rider, 1991.

Prager, Marcia. *The Path of Blessing.* New York: Bell Tower, 1998.

Ruskin, Aaron. *Letters of Light: A Mystical Journey Through the Hebrew Alphabet.* Brooklyn, NY: Sichos in English, 2003.

Additional Perspectives

Aitken, Robert. *Encouraging Words*. New York & San Francisco: Pantheon, 1993.

——————· *The Gateless Barrier*. San Francisco: North Point Press, 1991.

——————· *The Practice of Perfection*. New York & San Francisco: Pantheon, 1982.

——————· *A Zen Wave*. New York: Weatherhill, 1978.

Barks, Coleman, trans. *The Essential Rumi*. Harper SanFrancisco, 1995.

——————· *Illuminated Rumi*. New York: Broadway Books, 1997.

Besserman, Perle, ed. *The Way of the Jewish Mystics*. Boston, MA: Shambhala, 1994.

Bly, Robert; James Hillman, and Michael Meade, eds. *The Rag and Bone Shop of the Heart*. New York: HarperCollins, 1992.

Buber, Martin. *Tales of the Hasidim, Early Masters*. New York: Schocken Books, 1947.

——————· *Tales of the Hasidim, Later Masters*. New York: Schocken Books, 1948.

Carlebach, Shlomo, and Susan Yael Mesinai. *Shlomo's Stories*. Northvale, NJ: Jason Aronson, 1994.

Cooper, David. *God is a Verb*. New York: Riverhead Books, 1997.

Encyclopaedia Judaica. Jerusalem: Keter Publishing, 1996.

Epstein, Perle. *Kaballah: The Way of the Jewish Mystic*. Boston: Shambhala, 1988.

Green, Arthur and Barry Holtz, eds. and trans. *Your Word is Fire: The Hasidic Masters on Contemplative Prayer*. Woodstock, VT: Jewish Lights, 1993.

Heschel, Abraham Joshua. *The Quest for God*. New York: Charles Scribner's Sons, 1954.

——————· *The Sabbath*. New York: Farrar, Straus and Giroux, 1979.

Kamenetz, Rodger. *The Jew in the Lotus*. HarperSanFrancisco, 1994.

——————· *Stalking Elijah: Adventures with Today's Jewish Mystical Masters*. HarperSanFrancisco, 1997.

Kaplan, Aryeh. *Inner Space*. Brooklyn, NY: Moznaim Publishing, 1990.

——————· *Meditation and Kabbalah*. York Beach, ME: Samuel Weiser, 1982.

Karcher, Stephen. *The Illustrated Encyclopedia of Divination*. Shaftesbury, Dorset/Rockport, MA/Brisbane, Queensland: Element Books, 1997.

Langer, Jiri. *Nine Gates to the Hasidic Mysteries*. New York: David McKay Company, 1961.

Matt, Daniel, trans. *The Zohar: The Book of Enlightenment*. Mahwah, NJ: Paulist Press, 1983.

Matthews, John, ed. *The World Atlas of Divination*. Boston, Toronto & New York: Little, Brown and Company, 1992.

Meade, Michael. *Men and the Water of Life*. HarperSanFrancisco, 1993.

Mitchell, Stephen, ed. *The Enlightened Mind*. New York: Harper Perennial, 1991.

Mitchell, Stephen, trans. *Genesis*. New York: HarperCollins, 1996.

Mykoff, Moshe, ed. *The Empty Chair*. Vermont: Jewish Lights, 1994.

Prechtel, Martín. *Secrets of the Talking Jaguar*. New York: Tarcher/Putnam, 1998.

Rahula, Walpola. *What the Buddha Taught*. New York: Grove Press, 1959.

Raskin, Rabbi Aaron L. *Letters of Light*. New York: Sichos in English, 2003.

Roberts, Elizabeth and Elias Amidon, eds. *Earth Prayers*. HarperSanFrancisco, 1991.

Sakaki, Nanao. *Break the Mirror*. San Francisco: North Point Press, 1987.

Scholem, Gershom. *Major Trends in Jewish Mysticism*. New York: Schocken Books, 1974.

Schram, Peninnah, ed. *Chosen Tales: Stories Told by Jewish Storytellers*. Northvale, NJ: Jason Aronson, 1995.

Schwartz, Howard, ed. *Gabriel's Palace: Jewish Mystical Tales*. New York/Oxford: Oxford University Press, 1993.

Shapiro, Rami M., ed. and trans. *Open Secrets: The Letters of Reb Yerachmiel Ben Yisrael*. Durham, NC: Human Kindness Foundation, 1994.

Sheinkin, David. *Path of the Kabbalah*. New York: Paragon House, 1986.

Shlain, Leonard. *Alphabet Versus the Goddess: The Conflict Between Word and Image*. NewYork: Viking, 1998.

Skafte, Dianne. *Listening to the Oracle*. HarperSanFrancisco, 1997.

Snyder, Gary. *Turtle Island*. New York: New Directions, 1974.

Sperling, Harry and Maurice Simon, trans. *The Zohar, Vol. 2*. London: Soncino Press, 1978.

Waskow, Arthur. *Godwrestling — Round 2: Ancient Wisdom, Future Paths.* Woodstock, VT: Jewish Lights, 1996.

Weil, Simone. *Waiting for God.* New York: G. P. Putnam's Sons, 1951.

PERMISSIONS

Grateful acknowledgments to:

Jason Aronson, Inc. for the permission to reprint from the following three works: *Nine Gates to the Hasidic Mysteries* by Jiri Langer (Jason Aronson, Inc., Northvale, NJ, 1993); *Chosen Tales: Stories Told by Jewish Storytellers*. (Jason Aronson, Inc., Northvale, NJ, 1995) edited by Peninnah Schram; *Shlomo's Stories* by Shlomo Carlebach and Susan Yael Mesinai (Jason Aronson, Inc., Northvale, NJ, 1994).

Jewish Lights Publishing for the permission to reprint from the following two works: *The Empty Chair: Finding Hope and Joy — Timeless Wisdom from a Hasidic Master, Rebbe Nachman of Breslov* by the Breslov Research Institute (Jewish Lights Publishing, 1994); *Your Word is Fire: The Hasidic Masters on Contemplative Prayer* by Arthur Green and Barry W. Holtz (Jewish Lights Publishing, 1993).

Threshold Books for the permission to reprint from *The Essential Rumi* translated by Coleman Barks. (San Francisco: HarperSanFrancisco. Threshold Books 1995).

Broadway Books for the permission to reprint from *The Illuminated Rumi* by Coleman Barks and Michael Green. (Broadway Books, a division of Random House, Inc., 1997).

Georges Borchardt, Inc. for the permission to reprint from *Loving a Woman in Two Worlds* by Robert Bly. (Georges Borchardt, Inc., 1985).

Putnam Berkeley for the permission to reprint from *God is a Verb* by David Cooper. (Putnam Berkeley, a division of Penguin Putnam Inc., 1997).

Farrar, Straus and Giroux, LLC. for the permission to reprint from *The Sabbath* by Abraham Joshua Heschel. (Farrar, Straus and Giroux, LLC., 1951, 1979).

TRO-Hollis Music Inc., for the permission to reprint from "Walk On" by Brownie McGhee and Ruth McGhee. (TRO-Hollis Music Inc., New York, 1962, 1966).

Far Corner Books for the permission to reprint from "Kindness" in *Words Under the Words: Selected Poems* by Naomi Shihab Nye. (Far Corner Books, 1995).

New Directions Publishing Corp for the permission to reprint from *Turtle Island* by Gary Snyder. (New Directions Publishing Corp, 1974).

RICHARD SEIDMAN is a long-time student of Jewish mysticism, Zen Buddhism and indigenous traditions. He is a a children's book author and screenwriter, and a personal and business coach. In 1989, he founded Friends of Trees, a nonprofit tree-planting organization in Portland, Oregon that is still thriving. He is also a former teacher of the deaf, and holds a black belt in Shotokan Karate. He lives in Ashland, Oregon.

RABBI RAMI SHAPIRO is an award–winning author of over thirty books on religion and spirituality. He received rabbinical ordination from the Hebrew Union College–Jewish Institute of Religion, and holds a Ph.D. from Union Graduate School. A congregational rabbi for 20 years, Rabbi Rami currently co–directs One River Wisdom School (oneriverwisdomschool.com), blogs at www.spirituallyinde-pendnet.org, and writes a regular column for *Spirituality & Health* magazine called "Roadside Assistance for the Spiritual Traveler." His newest book is *Embracing the Divine Feminine: The Song of Songs Annotated and Explained* (SkyLight Paths). Rami can be reached via his website, rabbirami.com.

SHOSHANNAH BROMBACHER studied ancient Near Eastern studies and codicology in Leyden, Holland and earned a Ph.D. specializing in the medieval Hebrew poetry of the Amsterdam Sephardic-Portuese community. She studied in Jerusalem and lectured in Berlin and New York. Shoshannah has painted from an early age, inspired by Chassidic stories and Chagall works on her father's bookshelves. She attended classes at an art academy, but considers herself self-taught. She lives in Brooklyn, New York.